Alen Avdic

Shakespeare on Screen: Contemporary Adaptations of Macbeth, Much Ado About Nothing, The Taming of the Shrew and Coriolanus

D1826765

Alen Avdic

Shakespeare on Screen: Contemporary Adaptations of Macbeth, Much Ado About Nothing, The Taming of the Shrew and Coriolanus

LAP LAMBERT Academic Publishing

Impressum / Imprint

Bibliografische Information der Deutschen Nationalbibliothek: Die Deutsche Nationalbibliothek verzeichnet diese Publikation in der Deutschen Nationalbibliografie; detaillierte bibliografische Daten sind im Internet über http://dnb.d-nb.de abrufbar.

Alle in diesem Buch genannten Marken und Produktnamen unterliegen warenzeichen-, marken- oder patentrechtlichem Schutz bzw. sind Warenzeichen oder eingetragene Warenzeichen der jeweiligen Inhaber. Die Wiedergabe von Marken, Produktnamen, Gebrauchsnamen, Handelsnamen, Warenbezeichnungen u.s.w. in diesem Werk berechtigt auch ohne besondere Kennzeichnung nicht zu der Annahme, dass solche Namen im Sinne der Warenzeichen- und Markenschutzgesetzgebung als frei zu betrachten wären und daher von jedermann benutzt werden dürften.

Bibliographic information published by the Deutsche Nationalbibliothek: The Deutsche Nationalbibliothek lists this publication in the Deutsche Nationalbibliografie; detailed bibliographic data are available in the Internet at http://dnb.d-nb.de.

Any brand names and product names mentioned in this book are subject to trademark, brand or patent protection and are trademarks or registered trademarks of their respective holders. The use of brand names, product names, common names, trade names, product descriptions etc. even without a particular marking in this works is in no way to be construed to mean that such names may be regarded as unrestricted in respect of trademark and brand protection legislation and could thus be used by anyone.

Coverbild / Cover image: www.ingimage.com

Verlag / Publisher:
LAP LAMBERT Academic Publishing
ist ein Imprint der / is a trademark of
OmniScriptum GmbH & Co. KG
Heinrich-Böcking-Str. 6-8, 66121 Saarbrücken, Deutschland / Germany
Email: info@lap-publishing.com

Herstellung: siehe letzte Seite /
Printed at: see last page
ISBN: 978-3-659-54746-1

Copyright © 2014 OmniScriptum GmbH & Co. KG
Alle Rechte vorbehalten. / All rights reserved. Saarbrücken 2014

Table of Contents

To my loving parents

INTRODUCTION: SCREENING SHAKESPEARE

The number of films made from Shakespeare's plays has increased over the course of the past few years ranging from faithful adaptations of his plays to drawing on the Bard's material without actually performing any of his plays. Although seemingly not as popular as some other adaptations hailed by the popular culture as worth undertaking, Shakespeare still manages to bear considerable significance in the twenty first century and some recent films such as Michael Radford's *The Merchant of Venice* (2004), Kenneth Branagh's *As You Like It* (2006), Julie Taymor's *The Tempest* (2010) and Roland Emmerich's *Anonymous* (2011) have testified to this notion while resonating with the modern audiences worldwide. Screening Shakespeare in the twenty first century seems to be both a task that the film directors take seriously and a torch that continues to be passed on from one generation of filmmakers to another, from Laurence Olivier and Orson Welles over Grigori Kozintzev, Akira Kurosawa and Franco Zeffirelli to Kenneth Branagh, Baz Luhrmann and Julie Taymor. These filmmakers have transferred Shakespeare's plays from stage to screen with unforgettable results: from Oscar-winning British classics to Hollywood musicals and Westerns, from Soviet epics to BBC's modern adaptations, Shakespeare has inspired an almost infinite variety of films.

The answer to the question "Why Shakespeare?" must simply be, as Harold Bloom most poignantly put it, "Who else is there?" (Bloom 1998:1) Of all the screen adaptations that inhabit the silver screen the most enduring ones belong to Shakespeare and this was so since the very beginnings of the film and cinema. The first Shakespearian adaptation was *King John* in 1899 as a four-minute feature film (Henderson 2006:32) that set the place for Shakespeare in the realm of film. Just as his place was and is ever constant within the literature of the Western Canon (Bloom 1994:71) and the literature Canon of any country so too have the adaptations of his plays become a part of the Canon of popular culture. People used to go to the theatre to see a play written by Shakespeare and now they go to the cinema to watch Al Pacino playing Shylock in Radford's *The Merchant of Venice* (2004) or watch a feature film on TV that was adapted from one of his numerous plays such as in the case of the BCC production of *Shakespeare Retold*. The modern society has indeed a special place for this great playwright and all of his plays have been adapted for the screen which only testifies to what Ben Jonson famously wrote about the Bard: "He was not of an age, but for all time!" These words still hold true for most critics today. The timelessness of Shakespeare's themes continues to keep his plays fresh. He dramatized basic issues: love, marriage, familial relationships, gender roles, race, age, class, humor, illness, deception, betrayal, evil, revenge, murder, and death. He created unforgettable characters, from lowly thieves to lofty kings, who have become archetypes of modern drama, but remain people we can relate to. Both "of an age" and "for all time", Shakespeare is the defining figure of the English Renaissance, and "the most cited and quoted author since" (Garber 2004: 3). The very world we live in, think

4

and philosophize is, to use Ralph Waldo Emerson's words, "Shakespearized" (ibid). :

> But perhaps *Hamlet,* a play that from the Romantic era on has been established as the premier Western performance of consciousness, is too obvious a case to make this point. The Macbeths have become emblems of ambition, Othello a figure of jealous love, Lear a paradigm of neglected old age and unexpected nobilities, Cleopatra a pattern of erotic and powerful womanhood, Prospero of *The Tempest* a model of the artist as philosopher and ruler (Garber 2004: 4).

If Shakespeare's characters seem to us so modern, this is so because his language and his characters have partaken in the creation of modernity. This analysis is devoted to exploring the examples of this modern presence of Shakespeare in our lives.

In addition to analyzing contemporary audience engagement with Shakespeare, this analysis provides an analysis of the artists' respective methodologies of adaptation. The ways in which the writers and artists discussed here collaborate with and interrogate Shakespeare is of particular interest, as well as how they invite audiences to respond to and engage with the plays. The four plays examined in this study, *Coriolanus, Macbeth, Much Ado About Nothing* and *The Taming of the Shrew*, are analyzed in relation to their Shakespearean source texts in order to explore a question that is threefold: how are these adaptations interacting with Shakespeare?

How are the adapters asking audiences to interact with these plays? Finally, in the context of our contemporary world, what can these four adapted versions of the Bard's plays tell us about trends in Shakespearean performance within the context of contemporary audiences?

From a theoretical perspective, the question of adapting Shakespearean plays is intriguing: given that Shakespeare himself adapted a large portion of his plots from previous material, one should wonder what exactly is being adapted in the new adaptations. As the answer will differ from work to work, the reader is invited to consider the following titles of contemporary adaptations of Shakespeare:

- *Coriolanus* (2011), directed by Ralph Fiennes;

- *Macbeth* (2005), directed by Mark Brozel under the BBC *Shakespeare Retold* umbrella;

- *Much Ado About Nothing* (2005), directed by Brian Percival under the BBC *Shakespeare Retold* umbrella;

- *The Taming of the Shrew* (2005), directed by David Richards under the BBC *Shakespeare Retold* umbrella.

The study of adaptation, the practice of creating and producing literature, performance and art that maintains a sustained engagement with an informing source text or 'original' piece of literature, is a way of analyzing cultural, theoretical, and performance trends. This study draws on four distinctive contemporary approaches to Shakespearean adaptation and the way in which they reflect the cultural milieu of contemporary Shakespeare performance. Through first-hand observation, published books and articles, as well as performance reviews, this study constructs a cultural materialist analysis of four contemporary Shakespearian adaptations in order to understand how these artists converse with Shakespeare, as well as how they invite audiences to engage with retellings of his plays.

With the birth of the film as a mass medium it was not long before Shakespeare's plays were incorporated into the realm of the film and television: movies, feature films, musicals, westerns, science fictions films, epics, thrillers, comedies and other genres were adapted from the corpus of Shakespeare. Over the course of the years it became quite interesting how many adaptations of Shakespeare were made and one must simply ask how it is possible that this is the case? The truth is simple – Shakespeare wrote for a wide range of audience very much like television writers today. In the early days of TV, Shakespeare plays were seen on many drama series and this is the same in the twenty first century. Perhaps due to his reputation as "intellectual" or "high culture", today Shakespeare plays are seen on

TV and in the cinema. They have also ushered their way into our collective consciousness; they are a constant part of popular culture with numerous references in TV shows, sitcoms, cartoons, and science fiction. Hollywood seems to have found Shakespeare anew – his plays seem to be the perfect screenplays for Hollywood films. This is quite interesting to note since Shakespeare's plays could be observed not just as plays but as screenplays that pre-date the age of film. This ironic notion would mean that Shakespeare wrote screenplays some three hundred years before the birth of the cinema.

Directors and actors have adapted Shakespeare as long as his plays have been performed. Some feel that the adaptations without Shakespeare's original poetry, audiences are robbed of the opportunity to experience the cleverness, poetry, and majesty of the language, all of which are considered to be Shakespeare's genius. Others feel that modern adaptations do not challenge viewers as the original plays would and that they offer weaker plots and less complex characters. Yet adaptations often offer a commentary on the times in which they are produced and this was never truer than it is today: amidst wars and poverty that plague the modern world on the one side we have Ralph Fiennes' adaptation of *Coriolanus* (2011) and Mark Brozel's gritty and raw modern adaptation of *Macbeth* (2005) produced in the BBC's *Shakespeare Retold* series (2005); however there are also adaptations of some of Shakespeare's most celebrated comedies – again the fantastic BBC *Shakespeare Retold* series where Brian Percival's *Much Ado About Nothing* (2005) and David Richard's *The Taming of the Shrew* (2005) emerge as incredibly adaptive in portraying marriage and relationships in contemporary culture. Tragedy or comedy, Shakespeare's plays seem to catch on to the popular trends of our modern society by reinventing themselves so as to be relevant in the context of the twenty first century.

Changes in language, setting, and costume help place the production in a particular time or style. The variety of adaptations certainly increases our ability to understand and appreciate Shakespeare. For example, the contemporary language and setting of Fiennes' *Coriolanus* is a relevant statement on the wars in Afghanistan and Baghdad as well as a compelling critique on the 1990s Milosevic regime in Serbia. Brozel's *Macbeth* is set in the kitchen of a famous restaurant where Macbeth is the chef. The subtle critique of Britain's obsession with celebrity chefs and equating the influence of a chef with that of a king also bears relevance. The comedies, on the other hand, seem to speak volumes on love, marriage, relationships and deceit - Percival's *Much Ado About Nothing* and Richard's *The Taming of the Shrew* seem to stress this idea very potently with subtle references to the Bard himself or his work. The language in Brozel's *Macbeth,* Percival's *Much Ado About Nothing* and Richard's *The Taming of the Shrew* – in all the BBC TV series *Shakespeare Retold* for that matter – is well written, incredibly modern and up to date with the contemporary culture's demands. Only does Ralph Fiennes in his modern epic *Coriolanus* retain the Shakespearian language that, although the setting of the film is a contemporary one, still echoes with uncanny modernity.

Harold Bloom in his book *The Western Canon* claimed that of all the writers in the history of the world Shakespeare is the most relevant and that his plays have had the most impact and that "he (Shakespeare) is the Western Canon" (Bloom 1994:71)

It is therefore no surprise that new adaptations continue to allow new audiences to be drawn in by Shakespeare's characters and themes. The seeming absence of theology and ideology thus leaves place for all the *underlying* theologies and ideologies to interpolate the canon of Shakespearian adaptations and to make them constantly new while keeping in tact the fundamental themes and motifs that are embedded in the plays. The directors such as Fiennes, Brozel, Percival and Richard seem to have found the recipe as did Olivier, Wells, Kozintsev, Zeffirelli and Kurosawa before them: to make a completely new piece of work while preserving the original play.

Bearing all this in mind, this thesis will attempt to elucidate on the phenomenon of the modern Shakespearian adaptation. The focus will be set on the above mentioned four popular adaptations: Fiennes' *Coriolanus* (2011), Brozel's *Macbeth* (2005), Percival's *Much Ado About Nothing* (2005) and Richard's *The Taming of the Shrew* (2005). This analysis will be undertaken in the light of cultural materialist practice and with the stress on the contemporary sociopolitical as well as cultural aspects that are imbued within these adaptations. Since Shakespeare on screen is a topic that is quite extensive, there is a need to shed light on the theoretical overview of the most important adaptations of the Bard wherein the bond between television and Shakespeare became as strong and resilient as it is today. Following the overview of the most acknowledged Shakespearian adaptations, the relation between cultural materialism, the visual method and the contemporary adaptation will be commented on with the accent on the methodology of adapting Shakespeare that are at the focus of the thesis. This theoretical introduction will clarify the manner and the methodology of engaging with a topic that is as popular as it is contemporary in itself as Shakespeare on screen is.

Upon finishing the theoretical section of the thesis, the focus will imminently shift on the analysis section of the four adaptations: Fiennes' *Coriolanus* (2011), Brozel's *Macbeth* (2005), Percival's *Much Ado About Nothing* (2005) and Richard's *The Taming of the Shrew* (2005). For the sake of a more insightful and an easier analysis, this section is divided into two parts: the first part deals with the analysis of the tragedies - Fiennes' *Coriolanus* (2011) and Brozel's *Macbeth* (2005) wherein these two adaptations will be analyzed within the sociopolitical context of our contemporary world; and the second part which deals with the comedies - Percival's *Much Ado About Nothing* (2005) and Richard's *The Taming of the Shrew* (2005), where these two adaptations will be compared and contrasted in relation to their themes and motifs. The methodology of examining these four adaptations is closely linked with the theory of cultural materialism and it will be through the lenses of this theory that the aforementioned adaptations are reviewed and contemplated.

11

A Theoretical Overview of Shakespearian Adaptations

The romantic comedy Shakespeare in Love (1998) wittily puts the dramatist into the world of show business. Shakespeare's relationship with the theatre manager, Henslowe – and through him with 'the money' – is the occasion for a multitude of jokes referring to the entertainment industry of   late   sixteenth-century London in terms of its equivalent four hundred years later. In one moment of crisis Henslowe is even on the point of giving birth to a great cliché. 'The show must . . .' he starts, and Shakespeare completes the phrase by urging him impatiently to 'Go on.' The moment passes, unnoticed by either of them. The tension between the artist and the marketplace has always been a good source of humor in drama and fiction and on film, and the story is usually told in terms of the crassness of the producers and the crushed idealism of the 'creative' department. This is true to the experience of many artists, not least those writers and directors who worked in Hollywood at the height of the studios' powers. (Jackson 2000:1)

The entertainment industry, as Jackson notes is a site of a struggle between the artist and the marketplace. The marketplace is the audience and the product is the play or the adaptation thereof; they coexist both on and off the stage or the silver screen. With the emergence of the film there was a clear intent to make this bond between the artist and the marketplace stronger:

> Signaling a break not only with photography but also with the artificial reality of the stage, the moving pictures, as Charles Frohman observed as early as 1896, "make us believe that we see actual living nature", declaring henceforth that "the dead things of the stage must go". At its inception, then, cinema produced the equivalent of "a cult of life". Indeed its novel ability to store time in moving images led to the preoccupation with early innovators with filming the activities of everyday life. But as films entered mass culture, they produced not only fascination, but apprehension. Rather than replacing "dead things of the stage" with "actual living nature", cinema replaced living actors with ghostly, flickering shadows on the screen, eliciting a sense of emptiness and death more that the experience of a "real" life it promised to contain. The proliferation of these barren images (…) contributed to the feeling of trauma that would characterize modernity as a barrage of disconnected and frequently disturbing images. Partly in response to this threat, the cinema developed the narrative – its dominant form: the use of selective images in succession to create an illusion of consistent dramatic action. (Starks and Lehmann 2002:9-10)

This is Shakespeare entering the cinematic stage. His plays had already been intricately woven into every fabric of Anglo-American culture (Starks and Lehmann 2002:10). Indeed it would be difficult to speak about the history of cinema without mentioning Shakespeare, for Shakespeare has been linked with the cinema and the film since its inception (ibid). Shakespeare, in a way, wrote for films, claimed Laurence Olivier (Cartmell 2000: 21). The film, being a social medium addresses the group, rather than individual participation (Holderness 2002: 6), served as a prefect vehicle for Shakespeare to enter the realm of cinema. Shakespeare officially entered the motion pictures in September 1899 when segments of Shakespeare's *King John* were filmed by Sir Herbert Beerbohm Tree (Henderson 2006:32). This was a milestone in the adaptations of Shakespeare's plays. The role of film and, in particular, television will be of great importance when screening Shakespeare in the future because it has managed very early to incorporate itself into the rhythms of social life:

> Television operates as a medium of collective participation within the fundamental social institution (family) and within the basic space of social living (home). Secondly, television is a universal medium to a far greater extent than the theatre or even literacy; as an oral and a visual form it is accessible even to the unlettered, its complex visual dialect easier to learn than spoken or written language. It can therefore claim, more than any other cultural form, to be a national communication medium. (Holderness 2002: 7)

As the century progressed and talking pictures replaced the silent film, new techniques revolutionized the film, television and the cinema which split into modernist art distinctions of 'hig' art cinema and 'popular' movie entertainment although this distinction did not always hold (Starks and Lehmann 2002: 12). In the fashion of cultural materialism, culture does not limit itself to 'high culture' but includes all forms of culture like television, popular music and film. Directors like Orson Welles and Laurence Olivier appropriated and adapted Shakespeare for the avant-garde "high" art cinema although Shakespeare proved to be quite profitable in "popular" adaptations as well from Samuel Taylor's *The Taming of the Shrew*[1](1929) to Franco Zeffirelli's box office hit *Romeo and Juliet* (1968). This distinction between 'high' and 'low' entertainment became institutionalized in the 1950s through the 1970s (ibid).

Deborah Cartmell in her book *Interpreting Shakespeare on Screen* addresses the history of the great Bard's plays adapted to the silver screen by claiming that it was Laurence Olivier's *Henry V* (1944) that succeeded to blend 'high' and 'low' culture, converting academics to cinema and the 'uneducated' to Shakespeare (Cartmell 2000: 21). This movie invented the modern Shakespeare film (Rothwell 2004: 50):

> Laurence Olivier's early version was not just his first Shakespeare adaptation as a director and producer; it also set new standards by making conscious use of the particular advantages of the film, thereby bringing the Bard's work to a mass audience – in Technicolor! (Mueller 2005: 228)

---

[1] This was Hollywood's first full length Shakespearian film (Stark and Lehmann 2002: 12)

The importance of Olivier's work is that his three Shakespearian adaptations – *Henry V* (1944), *Hamlet*[2] (1948) and *Richard III* (1955) were hailed as being "simultaneously Shakespearian and totally cinematic" (Schneider 2003: 202). In *Richard III* Olivier made the villainous king not merely meditate upon his vicious scheming but, notably "in terms of the relation of the theater to the cinema, Richard talks to the audience all the time, which is the absolute audience approach, not meditation" (Jackson 2000: 59). In a similar manner, Orson Welles, after establishing his name in Hollywood with his master piece *Citizen Kane,* also followed Olivier's cinematic excursions with his adaptations of *Macbeth* (1948) and *Othello* (1952). It is no surprise that Welles' films were and still are compared to Olivier's and Welles, along with several other directors will eventually become a part of the canon of Shakespeare on Screen:

> Olivier's films must be central among those Lawrence Guntner identified as having become a kind of 'Great Tradition of Shakespeare on Film', privileging the films directed by Olivier, Welles, Kurosawa, Kozintzev, Polanski and Zeffirelli. One reason for the status accorded to these films is that their source plays are the best tragedies with their strong story lines, large-scale characters and symbolic dimension which generate a powerful cinematic imagery on the big screen. (Jackson 2000: 171)

---

[2] Olivier's *Hamlet* earned critical acclaim with the film both movie goers as well as with the critics. Olivier received an Academy Award for best leading actor in *Hamlet*. The movie waso also awarded with Oscars for best art direction (black and white) and best costumes (black and white) (Mueller 2005: 557)

Welles's *Macbeth* (1948) was significant as a turning point in Shakespeare cinematic adaptation: "Its major effect on the critical response was to confront critics with a new territory of adaptive endeavor which had to be accommodated" (Davies 1988: 5). The common characteristic of Welles' adaptations – *Macbeth* (1948) as well as his later adaptation of *Othello* (1952) – the common trait between these two adaptations is that in both of his films Welles carefully engages with Shakespeare's emphasis "upon the need to tell and retell the story" (Mason, qtd. in Jackson 2000: 193) His films acknowledge the narrative imperative is the plays' performance and their method (ibid). Welles' *Macbeth* will be compared by the critics with the much acclaimed Akira Kurosawa's adaptation of *Macbeth* titled *Throne of Blood* (1957) wherein the above mentioned method of guiding the narrative is chiseled by Kurosawa to near perfection:

> Akira Kurosawa's adaptation of *Macbeth* titled *Throne of Blood* (1957) is the most complete translation of Shakespeare on film. The text is abandoned altogether, the action is shifted from medieval Scotland to feudal Japan; a western renaissance tragedy becomes an Oriental samurai epic. The film displays a militaristic society with an elaborate code of loyalty expressed in conventionalized social rituals (Holderness 2002: 64).

Certainly the most popular nowadays of Welles' Shakespearian films is his 1966 adaptation of Shakespeare's *Henry IV* titled *Chimes at Midnight* wherein Orson plays the role of Falstaff; the entire film is told from the point of view of his character which allows an incredible insight into one of Shakespeare's most complex and witty characters: "Shakespeare's comedy was never as a gloriously performed as it was in this Welles' adaptation" (Schneider 2003: 449). A more subtle adaptation of the same play will ensue in the 1991 Gus Van Sant adaptation of *Henry IV* titled *My Own Private Idaho.*

Shakespeare visited the musical in George Sidney's 1953 *Kiss Me Kate,* an adaptation of *The Taming of the Shrew*, and in Jerome Robbinns' *West Side Story* (1961) inspired by *Romeo and Juliet.* This appealing setting of Shakespeare into the youthful and energetic adaptations will spawn numerous teenage Shakespeare adaptations in the 1990s that will appeal to the younger audiences hence making the Bard popular with the teenager demographic (Baz Luhrmann's *Romeo+Juliet*, Gil Junger *10 Things I Hate About You*, Tim Blake Nelson's *O,* etc.) One of the most popular genres in the 1960s was the epic; in 1963 Joseph L. Mankewicz's, who earlier adapted *Julius Caesar* (1953), starring Marlon Brando, returned to this genre with his grandiose epic *Cleopatra* (1963) starring Elizabeth Taylor and the film received high acclaim for "its visual splendor and mesmerizing opulence" (Mueller 2003: 171). Along with a compelling modernistic interpretation in Roman Polanski's gloomy version of *The Tragedy of Macbeth* (1971) other highly cinematic versions of Shakespeare's plays followed such as Charlton Heston's *Antony and Cleopatra* (1972) which was much measured against Mankewicz's grand epic.

Franco Zeffirelli's contribution to Shakespeare on screen cannon continues to receive considerable commentary even though his last film of Shakespeare, *Hamlet* starring Mel Gibson was made as long ago as 1990. Zeffirelli has made three films based on the works of Shakespeare: *The Taming of the Shrew* (1966), *Romeo and Juliet* (1968) and *Hamlet* (1990) (Cartmell, quoted in Jackson 2000: 212). Zeffirelli exploits the visual aspects of his films as much as he does the Shakespearian lines (ibid). The visual aspect of the film becomes something that will bear even more significance in the period between 1960s and 1980s where there are some of the most vividly screened Shakespearian adaptations: Zefirelli's, Kozintsev's and Kurosawa's.

The Russian dramaturge Grigori Kozintsev directed a magnificent *King Lear* (1971) derived from the Russian translation of Boris Pasternak (Welsh, and Lev 2007: 110). Kozintsev made two adaptations of Shakespeare - *Hamlet* (1964) and King *Lear* (1971), both of which were and still are outstanding films as they are considered to be among the most praised films in and outside of former Soviet Union; "the worlds of Kozintsev's Shakespeare are concentrated in a reserved, very compact space" (Sokolyansky, quoted in Jackson 2000: 202) and this is what allows for the raw, sometimes even harsh and surreal atmosphere that inhabits Kozintsev's films. The gothic depiction of Kozintsev's *King Lear* (1971) will echo in later Hollywood productions – most notably in the gothic adaptation of *The Tragedy of Macbeth* (1971) by Roman Polanski, where similarly Polanski employs ominously unnatural silences and amplified sounds to create a sense of discomfort and dread.

After winning critical acclaim with his 1957 *Throne of Blood* (or *Spider Web Castle*), Akira Kurosawa returned with the adaptation of *King Lear* titled *Ran*[3](1985), a sublime work of art, wise and flawlessly directed (Mueller 2003: 396). Steven J. Schneider in his book *1001 MOVIES You Must See before You Die* (2003: 718) comments:

> Of the 1001 movies you must see before you die, *Ran* is definitely among the top ten. (...) The acting and directing in Kurosawa's adaptation ranges from brilliance to something resembling perfection; *Ran* displays the wisdom of an entire life in 'only' two hours and forty minutes during which time is simply suspended.

No Shakespearian adaptation before Kurosawa's *Ran* insisted so on the visual method of representation as well as on pure performance: "Some scenes in *Ran* have the qualities of paintings (...) Kurosawa loves these luscious tones, which shine so intensely that they seem almost unreal" (Mueller 2003: 396). It would be no long before Kenneth Branagh in his 1989 adaptation of *Henry V* exploits precisely the same aspects of representation and performance and the same will be the case with Ralph Fiennes' adaptation of *Coriolanus* (2011).

Kenneth Branagh's *Henry V* (1989) looks back to the golden age of Shakespeare on film of the 1940s and 1950s. The aspect of

---

[3] Ran means 'chaos', see Schneider (2003: 718) and Mueller (2003: 399)

Branagh's directorial debut that is most praised by numerous Shakespeare on film scholars (Mark Thornton Burnett, Deborah Cartmell, Samuel Crowl, Sarah Hatchuel and Kenneth Rothwell[4]) is "seeking to distance itself from the mannered, decidedly anti-cinematic BBC style of televised Shakespeare" (Cartelli, Rowe 2007: 12). Branagh, in fact, initialized a Shakespeare on screen revival by initiating more focus on more florid acting and direction, which he continued in his subsequent film versions of *Much Ado About Nothing* (1993), *Hamlet* (1996), *Love's Labor Lost* (2000) and *As You Like It* (2006) (ibid):

> Crowl, for one, contended that Branagh's *Henry V* jump started a revival in Shakespeare on film production, (…) in part to his demonstration of Shakespeare's marketability and successful integration of Hollywood styling with convincing reading of Shakespearian verse, but also owing to the naturalness, conviction (…) he brought to the role. On both accounts, Branagh was clearly modeling himself on two precedents: Laurence Olivier, whose own wartime production of *Henry V* (1944) was followed by *Hamlet* (1948) and then in 1955 his Technicolor version of *Richard III;* and to a less extent, to an actor-impresario, Orson Welles, who directed and starred in more idiosyncratic versions of *Macbeth* (1948) and *Othello* (1952) and in his pastiche of Shakespeare's first and second parts of *Henry IV* titled *Chimes at Midnight* (1966). (Cartelli and Rowe 2007: 12)

---

[4] see Cartelli and Rowe (2007: 12)

In the 1990s there was an imminent spectrum of possibilities best illustrated by the enormously different aesthetics, languages and narratives displayed in the well received Zeffirelli's *Hamlet* (1990), Peter Greenway's *Prospero's Books* (1991) adapted from *The Tempest;* Trevor Nunn's *Twelfth Night* (1996);   Baz Luhrmann's postmodern MTV-generation-appealing adaptation *Romeo + Juliet* (1996); Richard Locraine's *Richard III* (1995), which is set against a backdrop of a 1930s fascism and with a brilliant performance by Ian McKellen (Boose and Burt 1997: 3); Al Pacino's directorial debut *Looking for Richard* (1996); and Julie Taymor's *Titus* (1999) starring Anthony Hopkins. The allusions to Shakespeare in the popular culture of the 1990s were immense:

> Developments in cultural studies have made us relatively more attentive to patterns of Shakespeare allusion in popular culture. Mainstream films such as *Renaissance Man* 1994), *L.A. Story* (1991), *Last Action Hero* (1991), and spin-offs designed to appeal to younger audiences, such as *10 Things I Hate About You* (1999), *Shakespeare in Love* (1999) and Tim Blake Nelson's *O* (2001). Such back and forth traffic between high and popular culture has made us especially alert to "ghosting" effects of global celebrity. Those effects allow Mel Gibson's fiery star turns in *Lethal Weapon* (1987) and *Lethal Weapon II* (1989), for example, to migrate into the promotional field of the Shakespeare in film, in this case, Zeffirelli's 1990 *Hamlet,* thus generating an aggressive impression of the usually more cerebral and indecisive Danish Prince (Cartelli and Rowe 2007: 23)

The 1990s also established the Shakespearian romantic comedy film (Pittman 2011: 146) – Kenneth Branagh's *Much Ado About Nothing* (1993), Gil Junger's *10 Things I Hate About You* (1999) and Michael Hoffman's *A Midsummer Night's Dream* (1999) and, according to critics, most notably Baz Luhrmann's *Romeo + Juliet* which was criticized for being a production of "MTV Shakespeare" but later on defended as an "alternative, a popular way to satisfy existing markets (but appealing to teenagers, who must, apparently against their will, read Shakespeare in school)" (Walker, and 2003: 126). *Romeo + Juliet* was later claimed as "an aggressive attempt to claim Shakespeare for the MTV generation" (Walker, and 2003: 126). In a similar manner Gil Junger's romantic comedy *10 Things I Hate About You* (1999), which is an adaptation of *The Taming of the Shrew,* was set to appeal to teenagers with the premise that Katherine, or 'Kat', 'the shrew' (Julia Stiles) goes to a high school and has the same 'problems' as millions of teenager worldwide until she is wooed and eventually won over by the Petruchio-character aptly named 'Patrick' (Heath Ledger).

However, during this turbulent period of the 1990s there was also a clear need to take a step further in depicting the state of mind of that period via Shakespearian adaptations; Gus Van Sant did precisely this with *My Own Private Idaho* (1992) starring River Phoenix and Keanu Reeves where the issues of alienated youth is addressed by subtly deconstructing *Henry IV.* A few years, Julie Taymor will make a similar

23

step with her adaptation of *Titus Andronicus* titled simply *Titus* (1999) and starring Anthony Hopkins. The films that followed this thread of profound self-examination were the two adaptations of *Hamlet* — Zeffirelli's edgy 1990s adaptation with Mel Gibson and Kenneth Branagh's 1996 adaptation of his "lavish, anachronistic, spectacular, often majestic and magnificent and, at times, unbearably long adaptation" (Pittman 2011: 146) wherein Branagh both starred and directed *Hamlet* very much in the same fashion as Laurence Olivier did some years before him.

The rise of pop culture in the 1990s culminated with the 1998 John Madden adaptation of *Shakespeare in Love* which was showered with Academy Awards[5] because of its incredibly stylistic and per formative quality:

> Against a well-researched backdrop of Elizabethan theatrical life, the plot speculates about Shakespeare's private life, which in fact, remains a mystery to critics even today. The screenplay skillfully combines elements from his plays with historical fact and pure fantasy. But there is nothing dry or dusty about it, it's not only about the English theatre in the 16th century but it is also a radical modernization of Shakespeare. (Mueller 2001: 582)

---

[5] *Shakespeare in Love* won seven Oscars, including best picture, best leading actress and best suppotring actress.

The original idea behind Madden's Oscar winning film is that it actually does not draw on any of the particular plays but it reaches to Shakespeare's material. This is where we come back to what we claimed at the begging of the overview: the adaptation, just like the film for that matter, it is the struggle between the marketplace and the writer; perhaps nowhere is this better to be seen than in *Shakespeare in Love*. If Shakespeare would be alive today, he would have been a screenplay writer and a Hollywood star (ibid). This trend of drawing on Shakespeare's life and using it as a basis for adaptation will also be revisited in Roland Emmerich's *Anonymous* (2011).

Finally the 2000s have too seen their portion of Shakespeare on screen. The popular BBC adaptations that reigned in the 1980s and 1990s could not longer hold against the marching army of films on Shakespeare and therefore felt the need to reinvent itself anew. This they certainly succeeded in with the BBC's 2005 *Shakespeare Retold* series where the Bard's plays were contextualized so as to fit the frames of contemporary popular culture. Notable movies in the 2000s include Kenneth Branagh's adaptations of *Love's Labor Lost* (2000) where the play was transported to the musical with its golden-age-Hollywood setting evoking the genres of the 1930s and *As You Like It* (2006), which Branagh adapted to a Japanese kabuki[6] drama that resonates with the Elizabethan drama: namely, kabuki has men playing the roles of women; there is wrestling in the play which Branagh exploits by having sumo wrestlers, the element of dancing – all well

---

[6] Classical Japanese dance drama

incorporated by Branagh, whose Japanese contextualized work can be seen as homage to the brilliant works of Kurosawa.

In Michael Radford's *The Merchant of Venice* (2004), Al Pacino, who directed the 1996 *Looking for Richard,* now returned to the Shakespeare adaptation and, indeed, excelled as Shylock:

> Pacino displays a remarkable technical mastery of the crisp, taut, repetitive invective (and sly irony) of Shylock's language and conspicuously avoids bending his portrayal to catch at modern sensibilities. (Crow, quoted in Burnett and Wray 2006: 113-114)

Screening Shakespeare became incredibly popular within the mainstream culture and it was only a matter of time before the BBC adaptations would emerge with the *title Shakespeare Retold* in 2005, offering adaptations such as *Macbeth, Much Ado About Nothing, The Taming of the Shrew* and *A Midsummer Night's Dream.* The fascinating aspect that these adaptations incorporated within their 're-telling' of the Bard's plays is a rather simple one, and one already recognized before them by the acclaimed representatives of the Shakespeare on screen canon like Olivier, Welles, Kurosawa and Branagh. It was relocating Shakespeare into a different context while preserving the essence of his plays. The most striking aspect of the BBC serial on Shakespeare, and the one that is the subject of this thesis, is the contemporariness of these adaptations – Mark Brozel's *Macbeth,* Brian Percival's *Much Ado About Nothing* and David Richard's *The Taming of the Shrew* – all of them being the topic of this thesis along with Fiennes' *Coriolanus* (2011), offer the contemporary view on Shakespeare's work that is embedded deeply within the popular culture and history that shapes and reshapes all of us. In these four adaptations, the grand Shakespearian heroes are portrayed as our contemporaries with problems that are easily identifiable and, indeed intimately close to our own.

Jan Kott in his book *Shakespeare, Our Contemporary* claimed that Shakespeare's reach on our lives is not diminished regardless of the centuries that divide our modern reality and his Renaissance world. This was never truer than in the case of the adaptations of *Coriolanus* (2011), *Macbeth* (2005), *Much Ado About Nothing* (2005) and *The Taming of the Shrew* (2005) for in these adaptations the characters are so realistically depicted that the quality of their performance has left the world wanting for more adapted works of the Bard's plays; and this yearning will be satisfied with the adaptations that will follow such as the screen adaptation of Shakespeare's history plays comprising *King Richard II; King Henry IV, Part 1 and 2 and King Henry V* in the form of a revived BBC TV mini series titled *The Hollow Crown* (2012) and starring Jeremy Irons. This latest project joins the incredible exuberance of the BBC adaptations, the characters bigger than life – wherein all is cloaked with the cape of modernity so skillfully that we are in awe when we see Macbeth as a chef of restaurant, Benedick and Beatrice as news anchors or Petruchio and Katherine set in the domain of modern politics. Even general Coriolanus in Fiennes' adaptation is a chief commander of the army of a contemporary country "calling itself Rome" where he is pushed by his ambition to his

27

very limits. Relocating Shakespeare like this into the realm of the contemporary world was never as thrilling and exuberating.

Relocating Shakespeare was also something Julie Taymor did in her 2010 adaptation of *The Tempest* wherein she cast Helen Mirren to play Prospera, the female version of Prospero which also contextualized the role of Shakespearian characters gender wise:

> Presiding over a motley, talented assembly is Helen Mirren as Prospera, the former duchess of Milan and Ms. Taymor's most provocative and persuasive act of revision. Switching the gender of Prospero — an aging wizard who is also his author's last and fondest alter ego — is more than a gimmick. When the character is a woman, a central relationship in the play, between the magician and her doted-on child, Miranda, sheds some of its traditional, patriarchal dynamic. Instead, a mother-daughter bond fraught with envy, protectiveness and identification blossoms into something newly rich and strange. (Scott 2010)

Taymor's adaptation was followed by Roland Emmerich's *Anonymous* (2011) wherein the popular Shakespearian controversy regarding the Bard's authorship was tackled upon. Emmerich's adaptation focuses on the count of Oxford, who in this film is attributed with writing the Shakespeare's plays, and the socio political circumstances that surrounded his life:

More importantly, he (Emmerich) draws on the Queen's own fascination with dramaturgy and poetry, which allows the film to dwell rather interestingly on the connection between art and politics ("All art is political, otherwise it would just be decoration," snaps Oxford). And most fittingly for a play about such great works, there are some wonderful performances too (...) and . Emmerich vividly portrays Elizabethan audiences and their visceral appreciation of the plays put before them (Wise 2011).

Taymor, Branagh, Emmerich, and Fiennes are among the last wave of Shakespearian resurrection on the silver screen and along with the 2005 BBC *Shakespeare Retold* series that inhabits the realm of television, we could say that the contemporary screening of Shakespeare has come a long way from Olivier, Welles, Kozintsev, Kurosawa to Branagh and this is the final set of directors and actors who exploit the visual aspects of the film medium as much as they did the Shakespeare line.

This theoretical overview of the landmark adaptations of Shakespeare throughout the history of film and television is important in setting the cultural materialist context in which Shakespeare on screen operated so far and up to date and it would perhaps help in foreshadowing where it will go from this point on. Our contemporary culture has expressed a yearning for the adaptation as a cultural phenomenon; Shakespeare is not the only writer whose works are being constantly adapted but he is, as Harold Bloom claims, its canon

(Bloom, 1994: 71); and the practice of popular culture is to put Shakespeare in the very center of the canon – in literature and, ever more constantly nowadays, in adaptation. The practice of cultural materialism is to contextualize the adaptations of the playwright whose characters are bigger both than life and bigger than the silver screen to a new era – the modern world. Within the medium of the film Shakespeare has found the vehicle capable of transporting his plays into our contemporary world.

Cultural Materialism and the Visual Method in Shakespeare

History, to a cultural materialist, is what has happened *and* what is happening now. In other words, Cultural Materialists not only create criticism of a text by contextualizing it with its own time period, but with successive generations including our own. The previously displayed theoretical overview of Shakespeare on screen is therefore important precisely because it contextualizes Shakespeare within the time period of the very adaptations it encompasses and, more importantly, it leads us to the final adaptations that are echoing in our contemporary world. Throughout the theoretical overview of this analysis there was displayed an ever constant notion of culture itself retaining vitality in Shakespeare studies, as Douglas Bruster (2003: 6) in his book *Shakespeare and the Question of Culture* addresses as developing into something we can call "cultural historicism". This cultural aspect of the adaptation imbues this study for we could clearly observe that there was a constant practice of appropriation of Shakespearian plays for conveying new meanings in the present; hence Shakespeare is turned into a modern conveyer of his text to the modern audience. Along with the practice of cultural materialism it is also necessary to observe the visual aspects of the adaptations, most notably the performance, for performance is closely linked to sign and the construction of meaning: "The visual signs the performance generates are not only the guide to its social and cultural meaning but often constitute the meaning itself" (Kennedy 2001: 5).

One of the main questions is: where is the appropriate setting for Shakespeare's plays? This question has preoccupies artists over the course of the twentieth century (Kennedy 2001: 4) and it continues to haunt every production of Shakespeare since then. Finally within the medium of the film, a most *performative* medium indeed, Shakespeare does find his place and the vehicle for the twenty first century. As previously mentioned, the focus on Shakespearian adaptations that will be provided in this analysis is one regarding *Coriolanus* (2011), *Macbeth* (2005), *Much Ado About Nothing* (2005) and *The Taming of the Shrew* (2005) – all of which were adapted numerous times before (some more times than others). One might wonder why is there a need to adapt a play anew that was already adapted only a few years before. The answer is simple – because our perception of these adaptations has changed. This is where the bastion of cultural materialist practice lies: cultural materialism embraces change and gives us different (changing) perspectives based on what we chose to suppress or reveal in readings from the past.

Shakespeare is the best example of how cultural materialism can change our point of view, and even our values, in regard to past texts. Many cultural materialists have challenged the relationship Britain has with Shakespeare and this becomes evident when we observe the latest of BBC's *Shakespeare Retold* series – all of which highlight the bond between Shakespeare and Britain. The need to claim Shakespeare for Britain ensues because of Shakespeare's grandness and his ability to *adapt* himself to any culture:

> The example of *Shakespeare Retold* (...) demonstrated how television now so very differently inflects concepts of the Shakespearian and reflects a broader cultural shift in attitudes towards and treatment of the canon. Richard Burt confirms this: "Shakespeare's decanonization and colonization has similarly transformed British adaptations on both film and television" ("Shakespeare" 23). The definitive has now been abandoned for the fragmentary, and textual purity has been replaced by an investment in what Burt calls the "essence of Shakespeare" – now understood to be plot. Burt elaborates on thus shift: "Insofar as there's a Shakespeare in any present adaptations at all, he seems to inhere in plot. The implicit claim is that the Shakespearian language is not universal but the plots, narrative conflicts, and / or character issues are" ("Shakespeare" 18). (Pittman 2011: 140)

Many may view Shakespeare in this regard as the prime *adapter,* and, fittingly so, he *is* the most adaptive writer in all literature.

Shakespeare's genius of writing is therefore constantly being adopted by cultures other than Britain. Shakespeare belongs to the world. However, the cultural materialist practice, that observes the socio-political context of the issue at hand, would claim that the questions of political nature are the reason why Shakespeare is relentlessly highlighted as Britain's national symbol. The issue of nationhood springs to mind when see that in these adaptations Shakespeare is equated with England; *Coriolanus, Macbeth, Much Ado About Nothing* and *The Taming of the Shrew* are British to the extent that their cultural heritage is traced within the confines of Britain; Coriolanus is a general of an army that resembles the British army or the UN; Macbeth is a Scottish chef in a restaurant (the allegory to highlight the cultural stereotype of English food is impossible to miss here); Benedick and Beatrice are news anchors (the allegory to their verbal skills from the play is very craftily adapted here); and Kate Minola from *The Taming of the Shrew* is set into the political domain of Britain (also aptly depicted as empowerment of women through politics). These adaptations claim the original plays for Britain. The jobs that the characters from the adaptations hold are also embedded into the cultural fabric of the British society; we no longer have 'the thane of Glamis' Macbeth but we have a chef called Joe Macbeth (note the casual and easily identifiable 'Joe', as in 'a regular Joe'). Furthermore, the verbose and delightful couple from *Much Ado About Nothing* Beatrice and Benedick are no longer noble lord and lady but they are transported into the world of television (hence using the direct source that helped screen Shakespeare for over a century) around which the entire film revolves. The characters from *The Taming of the Shrew* are also not far away from a 'modern' occupation; they are in the political system of Britain – again the noble titles have been, however, to a certain degree, exchanged for political functions. Even the most resilient and thorough of the four adaptations, *Coriolanus*, although retaining Shakespearian verse, situates its main character into the modern day; Coriolanus, a vicious Roman general, who is accustomed to the cruel and harsh battlefield of past ages, ironically finds his rightful place in our contemporary world that is as plagued by war and death as it was in Coriolanus' time. To sum up, we have a modern-day general, a few politicians, some news anchors and a restaurant chef – and this is, indeed, Shakespeare. This would probably be one of the greatest examples, in the studies of cultural materialism, which displays just how far the reach of Shakespeare has gone into our contemporary world. Due to the power of the adaptation, certain limits are erased and issues such as national and cultural belonging (*Macbeth*), addressing the political system (*The Taming of the Shrew*), commenting on the contemporary media (*Much Ado About Nothing*), raising concern about war and poverty (*Coriolanus*) are addressed. This is the power of the adaptation at hand and the reason as to why there is this constant need to resurrect Shakespeare.

Reviving Shakespeare in our modern world, it has been proven throughout the theoretical overview of the adaptation, is best done through the process of adaptation. By adapting a Shakespeare play, it becomes a changed version; it becomes *new* and this different (changing) perspective that imbues this adaptations gives us a *new* perspective; one that is apt for the context of our time. This cultural materialist practice is particularly true for the adaptations of Shakespeare because every era has its own Shakespeare and our modern world is no exception from this rule, as Marjorie Garber (2004: 28) observes:

> Every age creates its own Shakespeare. Another way of saying this is to observe that Shakespeare serves a wide variety of cultural purposes, from political nationalism around the globe to modern-day instruction in "leadership" for business and corporate culture"

With regard to the cultural materialist practice which stresses that culture is a constitutive social process and political process which actively creates different ways of life; Shakespearian adaptations similarly create and re-create new ways of life.

> According to Foucault, contemporary politics must take account of the notion that power is both restrictive and productive; and that it includes the power of the media, of film and television: Our present state of information technology and media shows that while politics and culture may have intrinsic ties to existing power structures, there are currently functioning strategies and tactics by which these forms of expression can call their own means in production into question in useful and even exciting ways (Keller, and Stratyner 2004: 7)

Every new adaptation of Shakespeare that we see on television or on the silver screen brings something new to our contemporary culture; it changes our perception of our popular culture and, indeed, it changes us. This is best done through the communications media, as we saw in Foucault, most notably the film and TV. Communications media have independent properties that impose themselves automatically; its function insists that its determination is social and always bound with social and cultural practices. The visual is an essential part of the theatre as well as the film; what an audience sees is as important as what it hears (Kennedy 2001: 5). The visual method in cultural studies has proved as a very useful way or rendering any text in the search of underlying meanings, motifs and practices. The visual aspect of the adaptation will therefore imminently contain the layers of the original text; in the case of the Shakespearian adaptation there will be the link between Shakespeare's original play and the adapted film at hand. However, in the terms of methodology of research, there are many more issues that the visual method can raise when undertaking a research.

Visual method is a form of research that uses drawings, maps, photography and film to elicit information. This research involves researchers going out and getting first-hand experience of the environment which they study. The main significance about the visual research is that it allows the researcher to play the role of the interpreter – to understand certain behaviors, experiences and texts by viewing the subject at hand. Therefore the control shifts from the researcher to the subject of the research. The visual research process is much more fluid as responses are spontaneous and often metaphoric (as in adaptations) and the visual method is also useful because it helps develop creative and analytical skills. The usage of this particular visual method is in establishing the relationship between the media and the audience (Gauntlett 2002: 254). For example, creative media artifacts such as videos, mock magazine covers, collages, etc are produced in representing the understanding of media audiences (ibid).

Creative visual methods are based on the understanding of art as an experience, that art is the way to survive, to help us understand the world and ourselves. It is a way to tap into the unconscious self through doing and thinking through:

> Visual fashions and gestural codes change swiftly, and are connected to places and time. This probably has always been true, though the extraordinary speed of communication in the modern world has greatly accelerated the cycle of cultural dissemination, decay and renewal. Popular movies, television shows and magazine advertisements only a few years old often look false or artificial because they were created to reflect or elicit a contemporary vogue, which, by definition, soon shifted. (Kennedy 2001: 4)

We ground the theoretical argument in a discussion of the use of creative visual methods in action research. They include metaphor, images using metaphor, visual representations of understanding, photographs, and digital manipulation of images. The use of visual methods can be a powerful way for individuals to conceptualize their understanding, making familiar experiences unfamiliar, and this is particularly true for the adaptation because the visual aspect of the narrative transcends the gap between the Shakespearian play and the Shakespearian adaptation for the visual provides researchers with a different way of seeing, and 'telling' in order to reconstruct ideas, understandings and make meanings:

> Just as the written work of history, particularly the grand narrative also attempts to put us into a certain context, so too the medium of the film intends to transport us into a particular context that is within the 'magic of the silver screen. (Rosenstone, 2006: 3)

Even if we are aware of the fictitious reality of the film, we conveniently forget it in order to partake in the experience the cinema provided. We suspend our belief in order to dive into the reality that the film offers because the film insists on the reality of the world it creates and analyzes:

> The worlds that films construe are so familiar to us that we rarely think about them. This, of course is the power of the film as a mass media. Films want us to believe that they are reality. The reality we see on the screen that is projected by the films is a

vision in its own constructed out of bits and pieces of images (ibid).

The visual method thus teams up finely with cultural materialism especially when cultural materialism takes on a whole range of topics – notably, sexuality, feminism, ethnic and post-colonial questions – to which other literary criticisms had traditionally given short shrift. To this extent, we can say that the visual method in cultural materialism forms a kind of bridge that helps pinpoint and stress certain practices that dwell in the domain of political, social and cultural aspects of our contemporary life. This is best done through a potent performance as well as a visual field of the theatrical representation:

Scene, scene painting setting, décor, decoration, design, costume, and dressing: many terms have appeared in English to describe what it is that constitutes the visual field of theatrical representation. Of all the terms available, *scenography* is the one with the largest and the most useful application, encompassing stage and costume design, acting, the arrangement of the acting ground and movement of the actors within it, and anything else proper to a production that an audience sees (...) Scenography can be thought of as a visual counterpart to the text; while the spoken dialogue of the play creates the verbal sphere of the production, the scenography creates the visual. Scenography should remind us most vividly that only the words of a play are insufficient for a thorough explication of performance. (Kennedy 2001: 12)

Scenography is closely linked with performance, a crucial term in the realm of adaptation; in Shakespeare these two aspects combine to highlight the construction of meaning in the new mode of cultural production:

> Shakespeare's plays were written as saleable commodities in anew mode of cultural and economic production and (...) his drama participated in the invention of a recognizably modern institution, the dramatic performance (Worthen 2003: 3)

This visual aspect of the dramatic performance allows for the adaptation to signify new meanings that are relevant in our contemporary world. Shakespeare is thus given a voice through performance and scenography – both essential to adaptation. By fragmenting Shakespeare through a modern adaptation within the confines of popular culture, new meanings are elicited and this allows Shakespeare to be voiced in *our* popular culture; most notably, the comments regarding the sociopolitical or cultural climate that will ensue from these modern adaptations will be much more relevant to the world politics in the 21st century:

> Shakespeare is a part our common culture: "Shakespeare" is one of the ways we communicate with one another today on issues of cultural seriousness – political, moral, ethical, social. Shakespeare the philosopher; Shakespeare the historian; Shakespeare the therapist; Shakespeare the moralist. This is Shakespeare as cultural shorthand. It is not an exaggeration to say that in the American public sphere only the Bible has the same moral authority. (Garber 2004: 29)

As Marjorie Garber in her book *Shakespeare After All* notes – every generation creates its own Shakespeare (Garber 2004: 3) and our modern generation has found the sociopolitical aspect of his plays most intriguing; the four adaptations - *Coriolanus, Macbeth, Much Ado About Nothing* and *The Taming of the Shrew* – are the ultimate comment on the contemporary issues in the world. Shakespeare seems as a perfect conveyer of meaning because, as Douglas Bruster puts it, Shakespeare is everywhere in our culture (Bruster 2003: 3-4):

His works dominate the curriculum in literature departments, his plays are regularly and widely produced, including, in the past two decades, the appearance of numerous film versions; the artist continues to draw on his his plays and poetry alike (ibid.) For Marjorie Graber, Shakespeare's cultural role is best described: With the language not of the celebrity market place of the analyst's couch: Shakespeare has been, and currently is "fetishized in Western popular – well as Western high – culture" (…) and if one believes Harold Bloom, Shakespeare is not only prominent in culture, but was primarily responsible for it – inventing, as he did, our way of being human.

Stephen Greenblatt remarked in his *Shakespearian Negotiations* that his way of reading "plays by Shakespeare and stage on which they first appeared" could be called "poetics of culture" (Bruster 2003: 4):

Leah Marcus in 1988 closed her book, *Puzzling Shakespeare,* with the claim that, "The Shakespeare that we want is not a man, a set of describable data, but an "ongoing cultural activity", a set of related, often competing activities which need to remain open in order to retain their vitality (Bruster 2003: 5)

Putting it as Bruster did (2003: 4), Shakespeare is the cultural author *for* us:

> Shakespeare, for better or for worse, has been, what Lawrence Levine calls "a cultural deity" (Levine 1988: 53), one of the privileged sites around which the Western culture has struggled to authenticate and sustain itself. Evidence of this struggle is as much to be found in critical studies that attribute to Shakespeare the invention of "poetic subjectivity" or, more egregiously, the 'human'[7] as it is to be found in the astonishing range of performance and textual contexts affiliated with the Shakespeare effect. (Fischlin, and Fortier 2000: 8)

Being more than a national icon, Shakespeare's potency of constantly signifying new meaning does not cease:

> The enormous box office success of Shakespeare films, both relatively straightforward interpretations and more freewheeling adaptations (...) suggests that watching Shakespeare is at least popular as reading him (Garber 2004: 29)

Every performance of Shakespeare is a new interpretation; and every new interpretation is a signifier of new meaning; it becomes a comment of our reality. The potency of adaptation precisely lies here: "Adaptation encompasses not only formal and cultural transposition of

---

[7] see, for instance, Harold Bloom's *Shakespeare: The Invention of the Human*

42

an earlier writer's source material but also the internal process of interpretative re-creation" (Martin, and Scheil 2011: 15). The following sections will deal with the representations of two sets of adaptations – two tragedies (*Coriolanus* and *Macbeth*) and two comedies (*Much Ado About Nothing* and *The Taming of the Shrew*) along with their contemporary and performative interpretations of our contemporary world.

The Methodological Approach to Shakespearian Adaptations

Since the four contemporary adaptations of Shakespeare in focus this study are relatively new and there is not much written about them in the domain of academic research, the very methodology of this study will use certain academic publications that draw on these adaptations as well as popular articles from newspapers such as *The Guardian, The New York Times* or *The Washington Post* where these adaptations were critically assessed. Apart from viewing the films and generating a range of ideas that could aid an astute cultural materialist critic, a substantial amount of time was spent on reading on and viewing of some of the milestone adaptations of Shakespeare so as to gain a wider perspective on the scope of popularity in adapting the Bard's work.

It was stated elsewhere in the theoretical framework to this thesis that Shakespeare, apart from being the most *adapted* playwright in all history, was also one of the most *adaptive* writers since he adapted most of his plays from earlier sources. It is therefore quite interesting to view these four adaptations of the artist who already adapted his work from some other source. It is therefore of pivotal importance to render the four plays examined here in relation to their Shakespearean source text. This methodology will provide us with an insight into exploring the questions provided in the introduction: how are these adaptations interacting with Shakespeare's original source? How are the adapters asking audiences to interact with these plays? Finally, in the context of our contemporary world regarding the modern trends and popular culture, what can these four adaptations comment about the current trends in Shakespearean performance within the context of contemporary audiences?

All of the four adaptations that will be problematized in this study are taken from Shakespeare's plays and made to 'fit' the contemporary world. The very manner of their adaptation has provoked certain cultural materialist scholars to observe them as gaining political dominance in claiming Shakespeare for Britain:

> If the Shakespearian meditation of the national is very much part of your persistent need to situate the past in order to comprehend the present then many would argue that that its neutrality on these matters has stood in question for long enough. And though

it is apparent that for some 'Shakespeare' merely continues to signify 'Englishness', the playwright has featured in construction, refashioning and articulation of a diverse range of other cultures and identities too. Indeed, Shakespeare has become the national poet of variety of countries in particular forms. There is, and was, a German Shakespeare; there is the contested legacy of contested Shakespeare in former British possessions; there is the post-national 'Shakespeare' who has served to focus debates concerning multi-culturalism etc. (Joughin 1997: 1)

Breaking the barrier of the national and establishing himself a part of the world culture, Shakespeare manages to influence our modern world and, although the adaptations that are the focus of this study do claim a British Shakespeare, that notion extends beyond this.

Shakespeare has become the main commentator on the state of our contemporary world. This will be seen throughout this analysis – that adaptations from his plays have generated a substantial amount of critical insight into our modern political, social and cultural reality. The literary theory that best engages with modern Shakespeare is cultural materialism. This theory will play the crucial part throughout this analysis of Shakespearian adaptations. Being involved with problematizing contemporary cultural practices as well as *performance,* cultural materialism is a primal methodological strategy that will attempt to elucidate on the various aspects of the four adaptations: "Cultural materialism is concerned with engaging with contemporary cultural practices (…) as well as accepting a wide range of 'textual' materials: materials from popular cultures, as well as performance" (Holderness 2001: 27).

The four contemporary adaptations of Shakespeare that are the focus of this study are, as previously mentioned in the introduction:

- *Coriolanus* (2011), directed by Ralph Fiennes;

- *Macbeth* (2005), directed by Mark Brozel under the BBC *Shakespeare Retold* umbrella;

- *Much Ado About Nothing* (2005), directed by Brian Percival under the BBC *Shakespeare Retold* umbrella;

- *The Taming of the Shrew* (2005), directed by David Richards under the BBC *Shakespeare Retold* umbrella.

Brozel's *Macbeth* (2005), Percival's *Much Ado About Nothing* (2005), and Richards' *The Taming of the Shrew* (2005) are a part of the contemporary BBC production titled *Shakespeare Retold* while Fiennes' directorial debut *Coriolanus* (2011) is also a contemporary retelling of the Bard's tragedy. In social, cultural and political terms, cultural materialism will be of great help when attempting to render these four adaptations through the prism of contemporary society; their criticism on culture, politics, economy, poverty as well as on relationships, love, deceit and fate will be elaborated on in the following sections.

When dealing with a work of art, especially one that was written by the greatest playwright of all time and one of the most innovative minds in our history, one must bear in mind that the adaptation of that very work may not contain the exact same amount of poignancy as did the original since the very process of adaptation means that something is changed, remodeled, made new. Therefore it is of great importance to grasp that the adaptations that will ensue in the following sections are precisely what they are – contextualized works of a genius and crafted so as to fit the realm of our contemporary world. This is where the methodology of research urges us to observe these contextualized works, these adaptations as attempts to situate Shakespeare within the confines of our modern world – a modern Shakespeare for a modern world. The following chapter will examine the first pair of adaptations – Ralph Fiennes' *Coriolanus* (2011) and Mark Brozel's *Macbeth* (2005). This pair of adapted tragedies will be analyzed in their relation to the original plays, the manner in which their contemporariness addresses the issues of power, culture and politics. Both plays containing tragic protagonists who are set against their fate; it is rather interesting to show that these two men, along with their ruthless and cruel nature, are fittingly made to be part of the 21st century.

CORIOLANUS AND *MACBETH:* MEN AGAINST FATE

This chapter will provide a cultural materialist analysis of the two adaptations of Shakespeare's tragedies – Fiennes' *Coriolanus* (2011) and Brozel's *Macbeth* (2005). Both plays and adaptations alike feature the two tragic warriors – Coriolanus and Macbeth; men undefeatable on the battlefield but flawed when met by their destructive appetites for power and political office. The issues of power and politics displayed in the plays were craftily incorporated into the adaptations; *Coriolanus* retains his undisputed status as a warrior but he is relocated in a modern-day country 'calling itself Rome' while *Macbeth* is relocated into a three star restaurant in Manchester thus where Macbeth is made the chef, subtly stressing his butcher-like characteristics. The cultural materialist analysis of these two adaptations will make visible the interplay of power and politics that had made the two plays into a few of most discussed in recent years.

Shakespeare's tragedy *Coriolanus* is one of his most politically oriented plays (Boyce, 2005: 79) as it depicts deep political conflict between the social classes. However, even though *Coriolanus* opens with civil unrest and features political machinations perpetrated by the tribunes, Roman political strife is not the principal subject matter of *Coriolanus* (ibid.) This play, although never a favorite amongst the Shakespearian corpus, provides a perfect political context for another story and that is the story of its tragic protagonist. The story of Coriolanus is first and foremost a tragedy. "It is a personal story of a great man whose greatness is accompanied by moral and psychological failings that bring about his downfall" (ibid). The fall of Coriolanus is not as famous the fall of Macbeth, the usurper of the Scottish throne and one of Shakespeare's most famous and tragic figures. However, there is a similarity between these two great warriors:

Like Macbeth, Coriolanus is a successful warrior who finds himself in a situation— here, the political world of Rome—to which he is temperamentally unsuited and in which he can be manipulated by others. Politically unsophisticated and emotionally immature, he can neither strike political deals with the tribunes nor resist his mother's insistence that he do so. He is reduced to blind vengeance, but she blocks him in that direction as well. Under these pressures, his great strength can only destroy him. His fate contains the irony found in all Shakespeare's tragedies: With greatness comes great weakness. Coriolanus' pride makes him great, but it also brings about his downfall (Boyce 2005: 87)

It is the human greed and ambition that like food nourish the basic needs of both of these warriors. Hence the imagery that revolves around food and nourishment is quite apt for both *Coriolanus* ('Anger is my meat' *Coriolanus* IV, 2) and *Macbeth*[8] ('My more having would be as a sauce / To make me hunger more' *Macbeth* IV, 3) as both are situated within their respective plays as warmongers, men ruled by their appetite for war. Their ambition drives both Coriolanus and Macbeth into their deaths. Whether ancient Rome or medieval Scotland, the universe of Shakespeare does teach us of the human potential for evil, as Charles Boyce claims: "It illustrates—though not in a religious context— the Judeo-Christian concept of the Fall, humanity' loss of God's grace" (Boyce, 2005: 350). As the stories of both Coriolanus and Macbeth unfold, both the Roman politics and Scottish courtiers alike fade away and the climactic confrontation in both tragedies shifts on to the fall of the tragic protagonist that meets its death from the hand of another warrior. The confrontation is no longer in opposition to social classes or political rivalry. Rather, it presents a conflict that is carried on within the protagonist's consciousness, rather than on some remote battlefield, for both Coriolanus and Macbeth are warriors *and* battlefields alike. The ultimate battle/confrontation will take place within the protagonist himself; it will be the clash of their pride and ambition; and, interestingly, with the psychological dependence of both of these characters on the strong women in their lives – Coriolanus' mother Volumnia and Macbeth's wife Lady Macbeth.

Furthermore, both Coriolanus and Macbeth are, in the adaptations that are the subject of this analysis, rendered through the

---

[8] It is not surprisning that food – related imagery imbues *Macbeth* since the 2005 BBC adaptation indeed relocates Macbeth as a chef in a prestigious restaurant.

prism of cultural materialism as characters that defy their fates. Both of them being tragic characters, inhabiting perhaps the darkest worlds in all of Shakespeare, are met by doom because of their appetites. Fiennes' 2011 film as well as Brozel's 2005 adaptation depicts this craving for power in *Coriolanus* and *Macbeth* respectively. The main theme of *Macbeth* – the destruction wrought when ambition goes unchecked by moral constraints – finds its most powerful expression in the play's two main characters. Macbeth is a courageous Scottish general who is not naturally inclined to commit evil deeds, yet he deeply desires power and advancement. He kills Duncan against his better judgment and afterward stews in guilt and paranoia. Toward the end of the play he descends into a kind of frantic, boastful madness. Lady Macbeth, on the other hand, pursues her goals with greater determination, yet she is less capable of withstanding the repercussions of her immoral acts. One of Shakespeare's most forcefully drawn female characters, she spurs her husband mercilessly to kill Duncan and urges him to be strong in the murder's aftermath, but she is eventually driven to distraction by the effect of Macbeth's repeated bloodshed on her conscience. In each case, ambition helped, of course, by the malign prophecies of the witches and this is what drives the couple to ever more terrible atrocities. The problem, the play and the adaptation suggest, is that once one decides to use violence to further one's quest for power, it is difficult to stop.

Coriolanus too is imbued with the pursuit of power and the desire to satisfy blind ambition. Though Coriolanus is himself unsubtle, preferring to express himself directly (indeed, this contributes to his downfall), he is surrounded by craftier, more manipulative characters.

His close friend, Menenius, serves as the perfect foil in this regard; for though he shares Coriolanus's aristocratic sensibilities and suspicion of the plebeian class, Menenius's smooth tongue and talent for compromise enable him to skate through the difficulties that debilitate Coriolanus. Menenius's counterparts on the plebeian side are the two tribunes, Sicinius and Brutus, whose talent for demagoguery and manipulation of the masses enable them to turn the people of Rome against Coriolanus – an easy task, given the hero's propensity for violent outbursts. Meanwhile, his Volscian counterpart, the great general Tullus Aufidius, is similar to Coriolanus in temperament but has a resentful streak that leads him to betray Coriolanus when he feels himself to be eclipsed in glory.

The most significant figure in Coriolanus' life, however, is his domineering mother, Volumnia. As a woman, she lacks the ability to achieve power on her own in the male-dominated Roman society; she also lacks a husband through whom she might indirectly enjoy public clout. Thus, Volumnia raises her son to be a great soldier, and it is her ambition, more than his, that puts him on the disastrous track toward the consulship. Moreover, Volumnia's controlling nature constitutes a major cause of Coriolanus' fatal childishness; and while his legendary stubbornness holds sway in every other situation, she alone can overcome it and convince Coriolanus to spare Rome and thus, unwittingly set his doom in motion. In this regard we may assume correctly that Lady Macbeth and Volumnia exercise their power to dominate over the protagonists of the plays/adaptations. This power of the female characters will be something that will be illuminated on when considering the power relations in the adaptations. Furthermore, the issues of nationhood and belonging which are closely tied to the politics and culture – as well as the issue of body politics which is something that will be discussed later on in this chapter. Also important to mention, and an integral part of the cultural materialist practice is the manner in which the modernity of Shakespeare and his creations, Coriolanus and Macbeth, have gained their momentum in the 21st century by creating not merely 'men against fate' but also 'men of emerging modernity' – models of modern men or, to use the famous phrase of the great Jan Kott, 'our contemporaries'. Before tackling all these aspects of analysis, there are several crucial similarities between Coriolanus and Macbeth that need to be stressed so as to make a clear bond between these two tragic protagonists; both of them inhabit ruthless worlds, worlds filled with blood and, shockingly, these worlds invoke our contemporary everyday life. The fate that Coriolanus and Macbeth challenge might be interpreted as challenging ideology for both of them were soldiers, among the best in all of Shakespeare, who, tempted by their appetites, decide to challenge the worlds they inhabit. In doing so, both of them show us the pre-destined trajectory of life that cannot be changed – all is pre-destined and therein lies their tragedy. The society rests of social conflict for conflict is the basis of society unlike harmony as many think. The conflict that rests in both *Coriolanus* and *Macbeth* is one that is external (the one where wars and political strife are fought vigorously) *and* internal (for the consciousness of the tragic protagonists is also a site where ambition roams uninhibited).

Coriolanus and Macbeth, both being the bearers of the titles of their respective plays, have stained the battlefields red with the blood that they have shed in order to protect and serve their ideological paragons. Caius Martius Coriolanus has dedicated his life in defending Rome while Macbeth fought for and alongside king Duncan of Scotland. These two characters would be the ultimate mercenaries from the point of view of the contemporary popular culture of today; both more war machines than men; both utterly committed to fulfilling their ambitions; both driven to the utmost limits of their physical and mental stamina. It is therefore not a surprise that both Coriolanus and Macbeth rank amongst other great Shakespearian soldiers such as Othello, Henry V, Hotspur, Troilus, Mark Anthony, Titus or Fortinbras. There are many scholars and theorists that would claim that precisely Coriolanus and Macbeth are *the* greatest of Shakespearian soldiers (with a possible inclusion of Othello). However, unlike other Shakespearian heroes such as Mark Anthony or Othello, both Coriolanus and Macbeth are rather gritty, raw characters that are quite able of exhibiting great crudeness and cruelty towards not just their enemies on the battlefield but towards just about anyone on their path (particularly Coriolanus with his rigid attitude toward the Roman plebeians). It seems that the plays connected with Rome, are amongst the bloodiest ones in Shakespeare. Blood flows in both *Coriolanus* and *Macbeth* just as it does in the Roman plays such as *Julius Caesar*, *Titus Andronicus* or even *Timon of Athens* wherein we have characters that invoke the tragic flaws similar to Coriolanus and Macbeth. Furthermore, both Coriolanus and Macbeth are ferocious, ruthless, proud warriors who have proven their military prowess numerous times in the battlefield and their qualities are mostly military. The worlds they inhabit are, in the words of Jan Kott (1964: 90), world(s) stained with blood.

These two characters, unlike others, are first and foremost warriors and their preoccupation with war might be the reason why their respective plays are amongst the bloodiest in all Shakespeare. This might also very well be a very apt choice to relocate the adaptation of *Macbeth* in a restaurant by creating the chef-butcher Macbeth. Very much like in any popular action movie where the protagonist leave heaps of corpses along his way to fulfilling his goal, so too do Coriolanus and Macbeth operate within Shakespeare's universe as killing machines that just about remove any obstacles that are in their way. It is their ambition that guides them, and ultimately it is their ambition that will lead them to their downfall.

The desire for power is manifested in both *Macbeth* and *Coriolanus* through unconscious cravings that are fed by the people closest to them. In the beginning of *Macbeth* the witches say onto Macbeth "Fair is foul, and foul is fair" (*Macbeth* I, 1) because "in their world, nonhuman and antihuman, everything is equivocal" (Garber 2004: 700) – all is double voiced. James's McAvoy's Macbeth in the BBC adaptation portrays a Macbeth whose mind is likewise encompassed by the three bin men who reflect his own appetites. In the play, Macbeth notably declares: "So foul and fair a day I have not seen" (*Macbeth* I, 3). We have here, within Shakespeare's play the double, equivocal foul *and* fair. Macbeth's mind, both in the original play as well as in the adaptation is shown as being in a condition where he conceives what the witches/bin men have prophesized. The echo of his appetite is unconscious, but it is there (Garber 2004: 700). The appetite for power is set when Macbeth exclaims: "Stars, hide your fires; Let not light see my black and deep desires" (*Macbeth* I, 4). The only thing he needs is a catalyst depicted in his wife, who enforces herself on him thus making his bloody decision easier. A similar unconscious acquiring of the appetite for power is present in *Coriolanus* as well. After Coriolanus had conquered the city of Corioles and deserved his noble name, the Senate approves him as a consul but he asks to be excused from the customary wearing of the gown of the Senate and the display of his wounds for popular support among the plebeians: "It is a part / That I shall blush in acting" (*Coriolanus* II. 2). Here too does the appetite of Coriolanus display unconscious desire for power. Fate imposes itself from the very beginning as the ultimate nemesis of both Macbeth and Coriolanus. Ralph Fiennes' Coriolanus in the 2011 adaptation displays his desire for political office regardless of the fact that he is not suited for such a job. From the start of the play he makes a series of mistakes not befitting a Roman senator:

> (Coriolanus) immediately creates a gulf between himself and the people that will never be bridged. He has the pride appropriate to a warrior, but he lacks a sense of ordinary social intercourse, let alone of compromise. He does not consider the justice of the commoners' complaints; he is simply offended that they should question aristocratic authority at all. His response is to suggest a massacre: "Hang 'em! . . . I'd make a quarry / With thousands of these quarter'd slaves" (1.1.189–198). From this initial outburst to

his final anger at Aufidius's taunt that he is a "boy of tears" (5.6.101), Coriolanus is incapable of flexibility. (Boyce 2005: 79)

Fittingly, his catalyst, as in the case with Macbeth, is a strong woman – his mother Volumnia – who continues to feed his ambition just like Lady Macbeth does with her husband. In order to feed their ambitions, both of these characters need to shed even more blood outside of their respective realms – they must become weapons against their own ideological paragons (Macbeth must secretly murder Duncan while he sleeps in his castle and Coriolanus must bring war to Rome in order to punish the people he ironically dedicated his life to protect). It is therefore no coincidence that both of these characters are surrounded by blood and dismembered bodies: foreshadowing of their imminent fate – which is one enemy that they cannot defeat. They are even visually portrayed as covered in blood which signifies their guilt (note the visual effect of the promotional poster of 2011 *Coriolanus* with Ralph Fiennes' face smeared with blood and the setting of the 2005 BBC adaptation of *Macbeth* in a restaurant kitchen with Joe Macbeth's hands constantly being bloody from cutting raw meat.)

Both the plays and the adaptations alike feature from their very beginnings two incredibly strong men who are depicted in a state of true heroism – men with great destinies: fighting, as is characteristic of Shakespeare's tragic protagonists at the outset of their journeys an external war (Garber 2004: 701). In fact, the blood that these characters shed in their wars is a constant reminder of both their heroism for defending their countries but also a foreshadowing of their imminent fall. With smeared blood come also the bleeding bodies and the manner in which the body is presented in the plays and the adaptations – the issue of body politics, a matter that will also be discussed. When we see Macbeth for the first time in the play, we imagine his face to be very quite like Ralph Fiennes' face from the promotional poster – covered in blood for Macbeth has returned from the war before King Duncan and Duncan famously asks: "What bloody man is that?" (*Macbeth* I, 2). It is important to note here in the play a very strong image of Macbeth, a man covered in blood who seems to foreshadow how the entire play will finish, standing before Duncan, the King. In *Coriolanus* we similarly have a very potent scene wherein we see a bloody Coriolanus who in the play ragingly asks his soldiers "Make you a sword of me?" (*Coriolanus* I, 6). This scene was adapted in Fiennes' movie as Coriolanus screaming to his soldiers: "Make me your sword!" As in the case of Macbeth, Coriolanus' blood-smeared face is a foreshadowing of his fall as well. The bloodthirstiness of these two protagonists is well visualized in Brozel's BBC adaptation of *Macbeth* in way that creates very strong emotions (Macbeth butchering the pig's head and displaying his skill with the kitchen knife to his fellow chefs).

The impulse to fight for glory – even more, to winning glory both in self-esteem in the eyes of others, feeding the ambition, fulfilling one's fate – has been implanted deeply within our species, or at least in the male gender, too deep to be uprooted before it grows again in many different soils. Whether dramatizing the traits of Macbeth,

Hotspur, Othello, Coriolanus, or other great soldiers, Shakespeare clothes his warriors in psychological complexity as well as in action. Their prowess in battle makes both Macbeth and Coriolanus men that are highly regarded in their respective societies although not liked by everyone. However, the clash of their unconscious cravings for power is met by their ability to make these cravings reality and so both Macbeth and Coriolanus are able to satisfy their appetites, at least for a limited period of time before they succumb to their tragic fates that loom large above both tragedies. As in Shakespeare's major tragedies *Hamlet, Othello, King Lear, Richard III* and *Anthony and Cleopatra* so too do the protagonists of *Macbeth* and *Coriolanus* exhibit tragic flaws that are eventually met by fate. It is the challenging of the fate that is deeply imbued within the fabric of both *Macbeth* and *Coriolanus.*

The most potent symbols of fate are the weird sisters in *Macbeth.* The sisters are called "witches" only once in the play, as opposed to being referred to as "weird" a total of six times. The term "weird," as we know, comes from the Old English term "wyrd," meaning "fate" so it seems pretty clear that they are in some way associated with the three fates of classical mythology. This is important to mention because the "fates" are supposed to control man's destiny and one of the major questions in the play revolves around the issue of whether or not Macbeth's actions are governed by his own free will or by his destiny. Fate had intertwined the life paths of both Coriolanus with Aufidius and Macbeth with Macduff. The two protagonists of their respective plays, their hands stained with blood, will imminently meet their end by the hands of their similarly bloody counterparts; Macbeth by his rival, the

Scottish nobleman Macduff ("Macduff was from his mother's womb untimely ripped") and Coriolanus by Tullus Aufidius ("A lion I am proud to hunt"). Both Macduff and Aufidius are given as the foils of the tragic protagonists. The similarities between them and the two protagonists are obvious – both Macduff and Aufidius are made to appear as parallel versions of Macduff and Coriolanus respectively and they are the ones that actually fulfill the destinies of Macbeth and Coriolanus. Macduff is at great opposition to the tyranny that Macbeth enforces:

> That way the noise is. Tyrant, show thy face!
> If thou be'st slain and with no stroke of mine,
> My wife and children's ghosts will haunt me still.
> I cannot strike at wretched kerns, whose arms
> Are hired to bear their staves: either thou, Macbeth,
> Or else my sword with an unbatter'd edge
> I sheathe again undeeded. There thou shouldst be;
> By this great clatter, one of greatest note
> Seems bruited. Let me find him, fortune!
> And more I beg not. (*Macbeth* V.7.)

The animosity that is displayed in *Macbeth* is one similar to the one exhibited in *Coriolanus*. It is quite clear from the beginning of the play that Aufidius and Coriolanus are, like Macbeth and Macduff, fierce enemies. However, unlike Macbeth wherein we have a rivalry that comes from within the Scottish realm, in *Coriolanus* the rivalry between Caius Martius Coriolanus and Tullus Aufidius is one that is external. The two are on opposite sides of the war: Aufidius serves the

Volscians, Coriolanus the Romans. Aufidius states that "if we and Caius Martius [Coriolanus] chance to meet, 'tis sworn between us, we shall ever strike till one can do no more" (I, 2.) Before the characters meet in battle, Coriolanus describes Aufidius as "the man of my soul's hate" (I, 5.). When the two are engaged in battle, Coriolanus tells Aufidius, "I'll fight with none but thee, for I do hate thee worse than a promise breaker" (I, 8.) Aufidius returns these sentiments, telling Coriolanus, "We hate alike: Not Africa owns a serpent I abhor more than thy fame and envy" (I, 8.) In challenging their surroundings both Macbeth and Coriolanus challenge their fate; Macbeth, from the very start and the prophetic vision of the witches/bin men wishes to fulfill his fate of reigning Scotland while Coriolanus in his desire for political office shows no remorse or compassion – both of them alike, behaving like soldiers on a battlefield. However, in challenging their own tragic fate, both of them indeed fall as both *Macbeth* and *Coriolanus* end tragically with the protagonist being slain by their respective foils. Macbeth captures this notion best in the play with the words "Blood will have blood" (*Macbeth* III, 4). In both cases a man-to-man combat will seal the fates of both warriors wherein both Macbeth and Coriolanus are slain by their foils. Macbeth is slain my Macduff while he practically welcomes death as a punishment for his misdeeds:

Lay on, Macduff,
And damn'd be him that first cries, "Hold, enough!"

(*Macbeth*, V, 8)

61

Coriolanus too, before being stabbed by the conspirators in the play – or in the Ralph Fiennes adaptation, being locked into a deathly embrace with Aufididius – he welcomes death as a liberation from the cruel fate that had lead to his downfall:

> Cut me to pieces, Volsces; men and lads,
> Stain all your edges on me. Boy! false hound!
> If you have writ your annals true, 'tis there,
> That, like an eagle in a dove-cote, I
> Flutter'd your Volscians in Corioli:
> Alone I did it. Boy!
>
> (*Coriolanus*, V, 6)

When one observes these two plays in this parallel manner as displayed above, we can tie the ruthless worlds of *Macbeth* and *Coriolanus* with our own contemporary world. The issues of power and ambition that are the drives for *Macbeth* and *Coriolanus* alike are but a piece in the giant puzzle of contemporary interplay of politics and culture. The modernity of Shakespeare's creations will display the everlasting game of politics and power that operates within the plays and adaptations alike. Both adaptations, just like the plays, feature the fall of the protagonist and the fulfillment of the fate that was present from the onset. The modernity of these new adaptations displays the crucial themes in the context of the modern world and the relevance of both *Macbeth* and *Coriolanus* in our contemporary world.

When analyzing Fiennes' film one we should draw on a cultural materialist practice that contextualizes the play in the modern time in which its new context sets it. Here the contextualization plays a pivotal role because *Coriolanus*, which was originally set in pre-imperial Rome, now becomes a play about contemporary man with a glance on contemporary issues of politics and economy. And contemporariness of Shakespeare's text is indeed still felt in the 2011 rendition of the play. The problem of "body politics" displayed both in the play as well as in the film is also a key ingredient in modern contextualization of Fiennes' film. The connection between the ancient Rome and "a place calling itself Rome" is clearly visible in the modern display of power struggle that is concealed behind the poor economy that dwells in modern Balkans that is plagued by horrid war memories and power struggles.

Brozel's contemporary BBC adaptation of Macbeth also includes a reading that encompasses the issues politics and power. Brozel's *Macbeth* is relocated into the contemporary world just like Fiennes' *Coriolanus;* the plot is situated in a three Michelin star restaurant with a lot of internal and external competition. However, unlike Fiennes' *Coriolanus* here the language of the adaptation is simplified and adjusted so that Joe and Ella Macbeth and the other characters talk and act from the perspective of the 21st century. The relocation and adaptation for the 21st century does not cease there; we have seen that the three witches are turned into sanitation workers – the three bin men and the same was done with the entire cast of *Macbeth*. Joe Macbeth is the master chef of the restaurant, his wife Ella a maitre'd while

Duncan (the King) is the owner of the restaurant. The relocation is finely tuned within Brozel's adaptation and this restaurant-setting gives a rather more intimate tone to the story of ambition and greed. James McAvoy's Joe Macbeth is a workaholic; a man who so desperately wishes to be on the top (to receive a new Michelin star) that he is ready to stake everything. His wife, embodied by Ella Macbeth (played by Keely Hawes) is the perfect catalyst for the ensuing bloodbath that will have the infamous ramifications *Macbeth* is famous for.

Coriolanus and Macbeth: Contemporary studies of power and politics

Because of the immense cultural materialist preferentiality for both adaptations – *Coriolanus* and *Macbeth* alike there is a need to focus on several key points as to capture the momentum of interplay between politics and power. Some of the key issues and concerns when rendering these two adaptations through the prism of cultural materialism are the power that the female characters of the plays wield – Lady Macbeth and Volumnia respectively in their plays; as well as the psychological dependence of Macbeth and Coriolanus on their love and approval. Furthermore, the issue of national belonging is another crucial aspect that manages to bear importance. Macbeth, 'the Scottish play', is adapted into a British film with the plot situated in a restaurant in Manchester while at the same time the restaurant owner Duncan is Irish. The melting pot of nationalities is present inside and outside of the restaurant and the most important stress is given on emphasizing the relation between Macbeth and Duncan. Furthermore, with these two Shakespearian plays being the bloodiest among his works, the blood and bodies seem to symbolically to represent the body politics that manages to bear a potent role in determining the power relations that are as well present within the adaptations respectively.

The manner in which politics operates within *Coriolanus* is best seen when set against the cultural materialist analysis of the play. This analysis can also be extended to the movie. The emphasis here is, primarily on the historical context that "undermines the transcendent significance traditionally accorded to the literary text" (Barry 2002: 122). The word 'transcendent' here roughly means 'timeless'. This is very important when discussing Shakespeare's plays since they have proven themselves 'timeless' in the sense that they are not limited by the historical circumstances in which they were produced. They are so much more than that. *Coriolanus* is a prototypical example of that claim because even when contextualized outside of the original Roman setting it still manages to retain its essence and it becomes perhaps even sharper in its problematizing of the issues of power and politics that are at play today.

The British critic Graham Holderness describes cultural materialism as 'a politicized form of historiography' (Barry 2002: 121). We can explain this as meaning the study of historical material (which includes literary texts) within a politicized framework, this framework including the present which those literary texts have in some way helped to shape. The framework of *Coriolanus* in Fiennes' adaptation is in a modern country "calling itself Rome" in which Fiennes has brought a powerful, challenging honesty to bear on class, political life and the demands we make on our leaders (French 2012). It reaches out in many directions, and in ways that Shakespeare could never have foreseen. It becomes a critique of modern society that extends on so many levels: social, political, economic and personal.

Coriolanus, being a drama about the relationship of authority, power and the emotions that drive them, in Fiennes' adaptation is reconfigured into a study of a modern Balkan-type state, racked with factional warfare and all the attendant cruelties:

Shot in Serbia and reeking of the recent wars in the former Yugoslavia, the film is as up to date as today's news, and indeed it opens as if we'd just switched on the TV to watch the latest bulletin from a state torn by civil strife. Here before us is Jon Snow himself as a newscaster, speaking Shakespeare's blank verse turned into breaking news and interviewing Roman experts on the current events for Fidelis TV. The hungry plebeians in jeans and bomber jackets are staging an uprising, demanding that the greedy, overfed patricians release corn from their warehouses. The quietly reasonable senator Menenius (Brian Cox) urges restraint, but his close friend the military leader Caius Martius (Ralph Fiennes) gives the crowd a tongue-lashing, and the police, their wall of shields resembling a Roman testudo, drive the mob away. It takes a war against the Volscian enemy to divert internal threats into external danger, and after the successful battle at Corioles, Caius Martius is given the honorific title "Coriolanus". (French 2012)

Contextualized in this manner, the movie becomes a bearer of many connotations with the issues of today. The greatest strength of Fiennes' film, however, lies in its clarity and intelligence:

He's clearly paid a great deal of detailed attention to how the narrative and the interplay of characters is to work – vital in Shakespeare films that can easily get bogged down in versification. (Pulver 2011)

The 2005 BBC adaptation of *Macbeth* equally shares the intelligence of the relocation of the plot as it features a refreshing take on the contemporary Macbeth:

Deeply influenced by Anthony Bourdain's book *Kitchen Confidential*, with oracular bin men standing in for the weird sisters, it brilliantly transposed the Scottish court to the fiercely hierarchical world of a Michelin three-star chef, with gleaming knives, obsessive handwashing and blood everywhere. First the kitchen, then the restaurant, then the TV show: a supremely witty transposition of Glamis, Cawdor, King. (Bate 2005)

This is something that firmly ties Fiennes' adaptation with the contemporary BBC *Shakespeare Retold* – the issue of relocation, as Margaret Jane Kidnie well observes:

The emphasis is on rendering Shakespeare's plays contemporary in terms of situation and social attitudes by incorporating into the action physical surroundings, material objects and behaviors that might be presumed to be well known to the BBC's projected audience. Characters send video messages by mobile phone, the get married in churches and pampered in spas, they travel by plane, bicycle and taxicab, they put out the garbage and they feed the children. Kidnie (2009: 105)

In Brozel's adaptation of *Macbeth* we perceive the transposition of the characters fittingly into the 21st century – and the manner in which the practice of cultural materialism operates within Brozel's narrative is rather similar to Shakespeare's original play. In regard to Graham Holderness's definition of cultural materialism as 'a politicized form of historiography' we can assume that, from a point of cultural materialism, Brozel's adaptation is an interplay of politics, culture and historiography. In the words of Jan Kott:

History in *Macbeth* is confused the way nightmares are; and, as in a nightmare, everyone is enveloped by it. Once the mechanism has been put to motion, one is apt to be crushed by it. One wades through the nightmare, which gradually rises up to one's throat.

Says Macbeth:
I am in blood
Stepp'd in so far, that, should I wade no more,
Returning were as tedious as going o're
(III, 4)

History in *Macbeth* is sticky and thick like a brew of blood.

(Kott 1964: 90)

Kott's observation of the historical-nightmarish aspect of Macbeth is one that was similarly caught in the 1971 modernistic interpretation by Roman Polanski, who in his film *The Tragedy of Macbeth*, similarly like in Kott's observation, has managed to capture this nightmarish, gloomy sense of discomfort. Polanski additionally used unnatural silences throughout his adaptation which were contrasted with amplified sounds hence creating what Kott would call confusion of history and nightmare. This is interesting to notice since Brozel in his adaptation uses silences in order to create a nightmare version of *Macbeth.*

Coriolanus too is cloaked in silence. When Coriolanus returns from his triumphant conquering of Corioles he is welcomed home to his wife Virgilia with silence, whom he then calls "his gracious silence". As in the case with *Macbeth,* silence plays an important role in Fiennes' adaptation as well since Coriolanus' wife (unlike Lady Macbeth) is given very little (or no) voice throughout *Coriolanus.* However, there is another character in Coriolanus that is not characterized by silence – quite the opposite, for Lady Macbeth finds in Volumnia, the mother of Coriolanus, her match. Just like Lady Macbeth dominates her husband, so too does Volumnia unquestionably dominate Coriolanus. The issue of power is well observed on the example of the relationship between Coriolanus and his mother. She dominates her son for she has so thoroughly bred her values in Coriolanus that he is psychologically dependant on her approval and cannot oppose her. As she claims: 'There is no man in the world / More bound to's mother' (V, 3). The relationship between Coriolanus and his mother is shown very vividly in Fiennes' film – their interaction that goes from a mother's loving care and devotion to her son to psychological torture of Coriolanus who is 'killed with kindness' by his beloved mother Volumnia (superbly played by Vanessa Redgrave). Volumnia is one of Shakespeare's strongest creations; a woman with unyielding values and a thirst for glory that can only be quenched by the bloody achievements of her son in battle. She manipulates Coriolanus and eventually she brings him to utter destruction for Coriolanus is a creature of her devising. She has commanding presence in the play as well as she does in Fiennes' adaptation where she is embodied by Redgrave as the Roman matron with iron will:

Early on she has a conversation with Virgilia, wife of Coriolanus and this scene is a study of contrasts; Volumnia is all blood and glory while Virgilia is human and restrained, worried about the fate of her husband:

VOLUMNIA: If my son were my husband, I should freelier rejoice in that absence wherein he won honor than in embraces of his bed where he would show more love... To a cruel war I sent him; from whence he returned, his brows bound with oak. I rell thee, daughter, I sprang not more in joy at first hearing he was a man-child then now in first seeing he has proved himself a man.

VIRGILIA: But had he died in the business, madam; how then?

VOLUMNIA: Then his good report should have been my son; I therein would have found issue.

Coriolanus I,
3, 2-6, 16-23

In this quiet exchange Shakespeare says more about Coriolanus than in all the battle scenes put together (Christ 2002:264)

Silences between Coriolanus and Volumnia on one hand and Joe and Ella Macbeth on the other are shown in both adaptations as visually compelling – this is where, as was mentioned earlier, the filmic visceral image comes, one might say, to life by vividly showing us the cold and unnatural relationship between these two pairs. However, we should note that the main relationships in *Macbeth* and *Coriolanus* alike also have certain aspects that make them some of Shakespeare's most intriguing and, for that matter, representative of marital values (*Macbeth*) or motherly love (*Coriolanus*). These are some of there reasons why it was necessary to make another fresh adaptation of both of these play in order to show anew the versatile bond between husband and wife; son and mother. The contemporary audience needs to see love between the Macbeths that transposes time or the overbearing love of Volumnia for her son – for these are the things the audience of the 21st century would be interested in seeing because we all can relate to having a mother whose love is smothering, or a wife for whom we would do just about anything. Lady Macbeth and Volumnia are, in this regard, given the archetypes of 'wife' and mother' respectively. The 'edge' on both of the adaptations is that the audience gets to witness the destructive love of both women that renders the two proud warriors helpless. It is very important to note that power in both adaptations is exercised by women. Stephen Greenblatt in his book *Will in the World* writes that the marriage between the Macbeths is "powerful, also upsetting, even terrifying, in their glimpses of genuine intimacy" (Greenblatt 2004: 137). The intimacy Greenblatt addresses is visible in Brozel's adaptation basically on every step of the way. The young married couple exchanges moments of verbal and physical tenderness which reminds us on the play wherein the thane and his wife likewise exercise their love banter just like any other couple:

> Here, almost uniquely in Shakespeare, husband and wife speak tie ach other playfully, as if they were a genuine couple. "Dearest chuck," Macbeth affectionately calls his wife, as he withholds from her an account of what he has been doing – as it happens, arranging the murder of his friend Banquo – so that she can better applaud the deed when it is done. When they host a dinner party that goes horribly awry, the loyal wife tries to cover for her husband: "Sit, worthy friends," she tells the guests, startled when Macbeth starts screaming at the apparition, which he alone sees, of the murdered Banquo sitting in his chair:

> My lord is often thus
> And hath been from his youth. Pray you, keep seat.
> The fit is momentary. Upon a thought
> He will again be well.
> > (*Macbeth* 3.4.53-55)

Then, under her breath, she tries to make him get a grip on himself: "Are you a man?" (3.4.57)

The sexual taunt half hidden in these words is the crucial note that Lady Macbeth strikes again and again. It is the principal means by which she gets her wavering husband to kill the king:

> When you durst do it, then you were a man;
> And to be more than what you were, you would
> Be so much more the man
> > (*Macbeth* 1.7.49-51)

(Greenblatt 2004: 138)

Brozel's fresh take on the young married couple of the Macbeths has equal value in representing them as – accessible to the modern audience. Just like in Greenblatt's observation that the Macbeths "are a genuine couple" (Greenblatt 2004: 138) so too do the Macbeths of Brozel's adaptation strike us like the average couple on the surface (with the common names – Joe and Ella) but this is only surface deep. Harold Bloom in his book *Shakespeare: The Invention of the Human* argues that Shakespeare, surpassing the obvious irony of having to depict the marriage of murderers, he indeed presets them as the happiest married couple in all his works (Bloom 1998: 518) and as being "profoundly in love with each other" (ibid.)

As with Coriolanus' ambitions fed by his overbearing mother need to be nourished, so too do the Macbeths plot to kill Duncan in order to take his place. Power and politics impose themselves in the murder of Duncan for "Macbeth's murder of Duncan was a political assassination and Macbeth was a popular hero because of it" (Orgel 2002: 164). The ambitions of the Macbeths need to be satisfied. In the words of Jan Kott: "Macbeth is placed near the throne. He *can* become the king so he *must* become the king" (Kott 1964: 90). With his partner in crime Macbeth obliterates the obstacle that was Duncan and propels himself and his wife into the heights of political office. This is how the surface of *Macbeth* is scratched deeper. Just like Coriolanus' cravings for power and political office, the Macbeths take what they want. Even though the title characters cannot attain political power alone, they are given their helpers - Lady Macbeth and Volumnia:

> The influence of Volumnia is the driving power behind Coriolanus and the play. Well may she boast to her son, "Thou art my warrior: / I hold to frame thee" (V, 3.), for she has bred in her son the pride that makes him believe that he and his class are incontestably superior. Yet Coriolanus is entirely incapable of dealing with the play's developments. (Boyce 2005: 80)

So too do the Macbeths, beneath their surface, crave power. On the surface they may be an average couple but the Macbeth and his wife are aware of their appetites. More interestingly they are aware of *each other's* appetites. Stephen Greenblatt writes about the relationship between the Macbeths as Macbeth and his Lady "inhabiting each other's mind":

> What is startling about this and about the whole relationship between Macbeth and his wife is the extent to which they inhabit each other's mind (Greenblatt 2004: 139). Greenblatt suggests that this couple has a special bond that is unique in Shakespeare:

When Lady Macbeth first appears, she is reading a letter from her husband that describes his encounter with the witches who have prophesized that he will be king: "'This have I thought good to deliver thee, my dearest partner of greatness, that thou mightst not lose the dues of rejoicing by being ignorant of what greatness is promised thee.'" He cannot wait until he goes home to tell her, he needs her to share his fantasy with him at once. And she, for her part, not only plunges into it immediately but also begins almost in the same breadth to reflect with studied insight upon her husband's nature:

> It is too full o'th' milk of human kindness
> To catch the nearest way. Thou wouldst be great,
> Art not without ambition, but without
> The illness that should attend it. What thou wouldst highly,
> That wouldts thou holily; wouldst not play false,
> And yet wouldst wrongly win. Thou'dst have, great Glamis,
> That which cries 'Thus thou nust do' if thou have it,

Andt that which rather thou dost fear to do
Than wishes should be undone.

(*Macbeth* 1.5.9-11, 15-23)

The richness of this account, the way it opens up from the first
simple observation to something almost queasily complicates, is
vivid evidence of the wife's ability to follow the twists and turns of
her husband's inner most character, to take her spouse in. And
her intimate understanding leads her to desire to enter into him:
"Hie thee hither, / That I may pour my spirits in thine ear" (1.5.23-
24)

(Greenblatt 2004: 139-140)

Macbeth and his wife know each other's innermost fears and desires
and this is something that couples nowadays practice. Even in murder,
the Macbeths are ferociously equal companions:

Whatever has led Lady Macbeth to imagine a bloody scene and
whatever Macbeth feels in response to her fantasy – terror,
sexual excitement, envy, soul sickness, and companionship in
evil – lie at the heart of what it means to be a principal married
couple conjured up by Shakespeare's imagination. (Greenblatt
2004: 139)

The manner in which the powerful women operate in both
Macbeth and *Coriolanus* is one of the key reasons as to why these
plays have gained more popularity. The issues of power and politics

are rendered very much through these two strong female characters. In the case of *Coriolanus* the modern component is seen in the aspect of how power operates not just on the political scale in Rome but also on a micro-level: with Coriolanus and his mother - because Coriolanus is both strong and fragile; a strong and mighty warrior on the battlefield but when his mother is close to him he becomes fragile. "This ironic situation demonstrates the basic theme of all Shakespearean tragedy: great strength is inextricably interwoven with correspondingly great weakness". (Boyce 2005: 80) This conflicting aspect of *Coriolanus* gives more depth to its troublesome character and, equally important – it brings the very character of Coriolanus closer to the contemporary audience. Likewise, the incorporation of the youthful couple of the Macbeths is also something that alludes to the 'freshness' and 'accessibility' of the play that is considered among Shakespeare's most complex works. Brozel's adapted version becomes a modern story of complex family relations (Kidnie 2009: 112), wherein "the impetus for 'Ella' Macbeth's murderous ambition linked firmly to a mother's emotionally troubled response for the death of a child" (ibid.):

> The solution to the literally riddle: 'How many children had Lady Macbeth?' turns out to be 'one' – a premature child who lived for three days. For Peter Moffat, the show's scriptwriter, the opportunity to cut through speculation about Lady Macbeth's cryptic reference to nursing a baby is one of the pleasures of this kind of project: 'you get to make a choice. I thought it would help our understanding of the character if we just said it – that she had a baby who lived for a while and died.' According to Keely Hawes (Ella), 'this information gives us an insight into why she acts as

she does. It doesn't excuse her, or make her a more sympathetic character exactly but it makes her more accessible to a contemporary audience.' (ibid.)

With the contemporary issues at hand such as war and poverty, the contemporary audience needs something that it can relate to. In portraying the characters of Coriolanus and Macbeth as political figures of the 21st century the writes of the adaptations have gone to great lengths to acquire the feeling of contemporariness in both films. In adapting the *Coriolanus*, screenplay writer John Logan (who worked on Ridley Scott's *Gladiator*, Martin Scorsese's Howard Hughes biography *The Aviator* and Sam Mendes' latest 007 adventure Skyfall) has sharply cut the text, removing the obscurer passages but retaining its lucidity and eloquence and providing a sharp, graphic narrative (French 2012):

> No attempt is made to make the proud Coriolanus into a vote-getter or crowd-pleaser. Whether shaven-headed and covered in blood from battle, smartly uniformed as a potential national leader or long-haired and bearded in exile, he remains his own man, a self-elected outsider. The only time he invites pity is when he yields to entreaties from his fiercely ambitious mother, Volumnia (Vanessa Redgrave), the very woman who has turned him into an uncompromising warrior. (French 2012.)

Ancient Rome is replaced by a modern state racked by civil war and political infighting where political machinations are "as clear as vivid, bloody battle scenes" (Maltin 2012). Fiennes' interpretation of Shakespeare's *Coriolanus* underscores "the soul-killing compromises demanded of democratic leaders, especially during times of economic turmoil; the power of the media to yo-yo public opinion; and the eternal tension between exceptional citizen and democracy's common men" (ibid.) While the play's saga of political leadership is at odds with the populace set in Roman times, the film unfolds in a modern city still called Rome, but shot in Belgrade (Pulver 2011) and drawing on the visual iconography of recent Balkan conflicts (Johnston 2012) – all grey combat fatigues, suffering civilians and rolling satellite news (ibid.). This is what makes the theme of *Coriolanus* still relevant:

> Fiennes's eponymous general is just the man to save the city from Gerard Butler's Aufidius and his Volscian assault force, yet clearly not equipped to deal with the political machinations of peacetime. Coriolanus may be driven by noble ideals, but he regards the public with barely concealed patrician scorn. (Johnston 2012)

Guerilla fighting from corner to corner, from one house to another in the Volscian city of Corioles is reminiscent of the wars that are raging in Iraq, Afghanistan or Gaza while Fiennes' character makes an uncanny presence; with shaved head and contorted face smeared with blood and dirt - "Make me your sword!" he screams to his troops while he finally seizes Corioles.

> For Corioles you might read the Falklands, Afghanistan, Iraq or Chechnya, and the battle is shot by cinematographer Barry

Ackroyd with the dusty, dangerous documentary-style realism he has brought to movies by Ken Loach and Paul Greengrass, and to Kathryn Bigelow's *The Hurt Locker*. Coriolanus becomes a national hero, but he's incapable of wooing the public because of his honesty, disdain for flattery and inability to compromise. The craven tribunes of the people (brilliantly played as shifty political opportunists by Paul Jesson and James Nesbitt) demand his banishment, and he's driven into exile. There he forms an alliance against Rome with his deadly Volscian enemy Aufidius (Gerard Butler), the guerrilla fighter with whom he shares a warrior's code and a homoerotic attraction. From this decision tragedy inevitably ensues, as he fails to live up to the necessary ruthlessness his actions demand. (French, 2012)

Brozel's adaptation of *Macbeth* also owes its screenwriter Peter Moffat a great deal since Moffat has managed to relocate the infamous thane of Glamis into a Michelin restaurant in Manchester. Here, similarly to Logan's relocation of *Coriolanus* into the 21st century, we also have the tragic protagonist dealing with the problems of everyday – he is the chef of a restaurant, his wife Ella Macbeth is the maitre'd while the role of the King Duncan is wittily replaced by Duncan, the restaurant owner. So conceived by Moffat's relocation, James McAvoy's Macbeth becomes much closer to the context of the 21st century. *Macbeth* becomes the integral part of our everyday life for Macbeth is stripped of all of his characteristics that make him 'difficult to comprehend' – he is not a nobleman, but a common man; he is not a warrior but a chef; and, most notably, the language of *Macbeth*, unlike the one in *Coriolanus,* is perfectly adapted to our contemporary world. Moffat wrote a screenplay wherein we have a character that we can understand – motivation wise and linguistically. The motif (provided by the prophetic bin men) goes had in hand with the workaholic habits of Macbeth but the language Brozel and Moffat introduce is the 'modern' style of the 21st century and Macbeth is heard and understood perfectly.

The usage of language in both adaptations is of pivotal importance since through language we understand the interplay of power and politics. *Macbeth* is interesting in this perspective:

> There were some glorious allusions to the original language: Joe Macbeth unseamed a pig from the knave to the chops and Duncan was known as "the old man" ("Who would have thought the old man to have had so much blood in him?"). Best of all, this was a creative reading that did full justice to the key that unlocks the motivation of the Macbeths: the death of their child. (Bate 2005)

Also, in *Macbeth* there are some short and easily recognized phrases are fitted into the modern dialogue (Kidnie 2009: 105) – Lady Macbeth says unto her husband that he "is too full of the milk of human kindness". The wordcraft of Shakespeare, as one can clearly see, at play in the adaptation as well and the rich usage of language does not fall short of being invocative of the original play. Macbeth is given some of the best lines in the play and his words echo his original character from the play.

The only character to rival Macbeth's wordcraft is Duncan, who recounts a childhood defining memory of his mother waking him before dawn to watch his father slip into the shed to butcher a sleeping Tamworth pig. When asked whether his father killed the pig in its sleep out of kindness, his mother gave him the truth rather than the answer he would have wanted to hear: 'The meat', she said, 'tastes better' (Kidnie 2009: 117.) This image, however, shifts with Macbeth's plan to kill Duncan in his sleep, the crime that seems a particularly horrific travesty of the art of butchery since in killing Duncan Macbeth produces meat that can only be wasted and not consumed.

The difference between Macbeth and Duncan is depicted in the adaptation as politicized form of cultural animosity – note that Macbeth is Scottish while Duncan is Irish; this animosity between the Irish and Scottish is depicted as mirroring Britain's cultural background. Unlike the play *Macbeth,* wherein we have both Duncan and Macbeth on one side, in the adaptation we have a divided country, or better, a divided restaurant with Scots and Irishmen on both sides. This brings back the notion of Marjorie Garber displayed earlier – her claim that Shakespeare's tragic protagonists are fighting at the outset of their journeys an external war (Garber 2004: 701). Garber's claim, in the context of the adaptation, becomes an internal conflict; it becomes relocated, very much like the very play *Macbeth* does in Moffat's writing, to the microcosms of today. The cultural materialist reading of *Macbeth,* very much like the one of *Coriolanus,* includes the notion of nationhood, of belonging. In *Macbeth,* we have the notion of a very subtle, almost invisible conflict between the Irish (Duncan) and the Scottish (Macbeth). This is amplified by the fact that the Duncan from the adaptation is made to appear quite differently than King Duncan from the play:

> Duncan is linked with light, day, and stars; Macbeth, with darkness, night, and 'a brief candle'. The pattern is elegant, pervasive and cumulatively powerful, the language clusters offering an almost subliminal imagistic counter–point to the ongoing dramatic action, as if the play's unconscious agency of the protagonists. Duncan's public pronouncement, conferring of the title of Thane of Cawdor upon Macbeth and proclaiming that 'signs of nobleness, like stars, shall shine' / On all deservers'. Moments later Macbeth, aside, speaks the the underside of the same figures: 'Stars, hide your fires, / Let not light see my black and deep desires (I, 4). Duncan wants the stars to shine, Macbeth wants them to hide. (Garber 2004: 703-704)

The opposition between Macbeth and Duncan in the adaptation, like the one in the play, is one of sharp contrast. There is no doubt that the Duncan from the play is a man much more deserving and noble that Macbeth. However, the image we receive of the Duncan from the adaptation, mirroring the sentiments of the cultural animosity of the British towards the Irish brigs about an image of a despairing Macbeth, a man who works hard only so that Duncan shamelessly reaps the fruits of Macbeth's labor. In Brozel's adaptation Duncan the restaurant owner is made not as appealing as was Shakespeare's King Duncan in the play. Shakespeare makes his king nobler and much more virtuous, while the usurper Macbeth is made more precipitate and vile in his designs (Garber 2004: 702). Indeed, in Brozel's adaptation Macbeth leads the kitchen and does all the work; he is committed to making the restaurant (the equivalent of the Scottish realm in the play) the best; alas all the glory goes to the 'executive chef' Duncan – whose real involvement never extends beyond popping on a white coat and greeting his happy customers. By taking credit for Macbeth's work, Duncan makes himself a very unsympathetic character which makes his murder in the adaptation easier to bear rather than the one of the noble King Duncan in the play.

The political relation Ireland-Scotland from *Macbeth* mirrors the relation Roman-Volscian from *Coriolanus* for the political issues at hand today. Unlike Brozel's adaptation, which is situated around England and has a rather intimate feeling because at the core there is the marriage between the Macbeths, Fiennes' adaptation features a political interplay of power and ambition on a grand scale. Seldom is there so much politics in Shakespeare that is as condensed as it is the case with *Coriolanus*. Perhaps its popularity nowadays can be attributes to the fact that the political, social and economic circumstances of today have finally found their reflection in the play itself. This litotic expression of relations between power and politics seems so apt for the Balkan region that it produces an uncanny resemblance to the regimes of power in the 1990s Balkans. It is so obviously presented before our eyes – the urban decay, poverty, run-down apartment blocks and ageing industrial sites – everything that we see in Fiennes' interpretation is reminiscent of the 1990s Serbia and the Milošević regime. Fiennes' choice to film in Serbs is in itself a stroke of brilliance according to Žižek (Haglund 2012) in the sense that it gives a considerable amount of authenticity to the film. It evokes the civil unrest in the recent Balkan conflicts – although the film can equally be relevant to the Falklands, Afghanistan and Iraq (French 2012):

> The heavy political emphasis of much modern commentary on *Coriolanus* is not misplaced, for the conflicts that spark the tragic hero's downfall are representative of the social clashes that constitute much of political history. The play stresses a theme that was important to Shakespeare when he wrote his earlier English history plays: the impact of immoral behavior in the ruling class on the peace and prosperity of all of society. (Boyce 2005: 80)

The Serbian Parliament building was turned into the Roman Senate for the production and "the protest scenes on the Senate steps unnervingly mirroring events that took place there during the war" (Hornaday 2012). Battle scenes were also filmed in the Hotel Yugoslavia, which was once the region's premiere hotel before it was partially destroyed by the direct hit of a NATO bomb in 1999 (ibid). Even the rolling satellite news that every now and then flash before us as well as the Volscian guerilla soldiers on armored vehicles evoke the horrifying images from the 1990s Balkan atrocities – the Volscian army that is heavily tattooed with religious iconography that not only represents their aggression and determination but also deep spiritual belief that their cause is just (Phillips 2012). On the other hand the Roman army is presented in a stark contrast – from their digitally designed fatigues to their state-of-the-art weaponry – they are presented as professional soldiers (even perhaps standing for the UN army in the Balkan conflict).

A quite interesting glimpse of the two Yugoslav men in *Macbeth* that Ella Macbeth uses in her plot to kill Duncan. This is a rather interesting involvement of the Balkans and the people from the Balkans as instruments of murder. This reference to the Balkan (presumably Serbian men) bears certain political resonance to the modern Balkans, and any war-ridden part of the world of today. The guilt here falls on Ella Macbeth for she had put the blame on the innocent Balkan men who were innocent. Fiennes' *Coriolanus* and Brozel's *Macbeth* strongly show that politics plays a crucial part in the lives of every each one of us, very much like Shakespeare's original play did several centuries ago. When one witnesses the impact of power struggles that imbue the plays and the films, one becomes very quickly aware of the fact that it influences everything, including economy of a given society and the individual's position therein. This is one of the crucial factors in something that operates within the confines of "body politics".

A body politic is a metaphor in which a nation is considered to be a corporate entity; A body politic comprises all the people in a particular country considered as a single group. The analogy is typically continued by reference to the apex of government as the head of state, but may be extended to other anatomical parts, as in political readings of the Aesop's fable, "The Belly and the Members":

The metaphor of the human body has been broadly exploited in western political discourse. In particular, adopting the human body as a model for the State has always coincided with the attempt to arrange political abstract "plurality" and to make it easily understandable: this statement seems to lie at the core of the most common versions of the corporeal allegory, such as Plato's psychocentric polis, Aristotle's organic political model and Saint Paul's vision of the Church as Christ's body contained in the first epistle to the Corinthians, all of which have strongly influenced the development of Western political thought. Because of its exegetic immediacy, the traditional metaphor of the body politic, originally coined by Plato and Aristotle, spreads in Elizabethan and Jacobean political treatises, and underpins many of Shakespeare's plays. In Coriolanus (1607), through the mise-ensce`ne of the well-known Livian "fable of the belly", Shakespeare dramatizes the old organological tradition, which finds its strongest upholder in John of Salisbury: the medieval author of Policraticus (1159) leads the traditional abstraction of the human body to perfection by idealizing the basest among physiological functions—that is, the digestive–emunctory one— thus providing his readers with the "most ideologically pacificatory among the organic and hierarchical images of society" (Spicci, 2007)

It has long been recognized that the concept of the "body politic" has a central role in Shakespeare's *Coriolanus* (Filling 2009). According to Filling it is a deeply political play wherein body politics holds meaning:

Coriolanus has been called Shakespeare's 'most exclusively political play', his 'only great political play'. William Hazlitt went as far as to say that 'Anyone who studies [*Coriolanus*] may save himself the trouble of reading Burke's Reflections, or Paine's Rights of Man, or the Debates in both Houses of Parliament since the French Revolution or our own.' The play has an overtly political subject matter – the conflict between plebeians and patricians (ibid.)

The conflicted relationship between the ruling class in Rome and the city's plebeians is often compared to the political situation in our own time, when landless and poor workers violently protest their growing economic poverty. Very much like the plebeians, whose major complaint is hunger, the contemporary working class of today too fears starvation as a result of bad politics and even worse economy. (Phillips 2012)

One of the most popular analogies when dealing with *Coriolanus* and definitely the one that makes the play stand out in the context of 21st century is the idea of the "body politic" – Shakespeare has the patrician Menenius Agrippa describe the Roman patricians as analogous to the "belly", the plebs to the "members" of the body" (Filling 2009). Menenius introduces his tale of the belly and the members by the admission that his allegory is threadbare (Borot 2007):

Menenius's fable of the belly is indeed an old tale (...) and stands on its own in the context of a Roman play. It is a cultural reference for those in the audience who went to grammar school (not a majority by far) and it contains enough echoes of the traditional body-politic metaphor to be reminiscent of its clichés to all the spectators. The stale allegory of the body politic is read through the stale tale of the belly. This reading does not alter the interpretation suggested here.

[...]

Your most grave belly was deliberate,
Not rash like his accusers, and thus answered:
'True is it, my incorporate friends,' quoth he,
'That I receive the general food at first
Which you do live upon; and fit it is,
Because I am the storehouse and the shop
Of the whole body. But, if you do remember,
I send it through the rivers of your blood
Even to the court, the heart,--to th' seat o' th' brain;
And, through the cranks and offices of man
The strongest nerves and small inferior veins
From me receive that natural competency
Whereby they live. (1.1.)

In Menenius' 'fable of the belly', collective cohesion, the hallmark of 'healthy societies', is menaced by the impending mutiny of the limbs, which can cause the complexional imbalance of the whole political organism (Spicci, 2007). If the political situation of the scene is considered globally (as does Fiennes in his adaptation), one can but notice that the citizens have material reasons to complain about famine, and to criticize legislation that was being passed. The citizens have something practical to argue against the senators. The members in the fable are not given such practical knowledge by Menenius who clearly confesses that, as narrator, he controls whatever the characters say or do ("I can make the belly smile / As well as speak" (1.1.) (ibid). The crafty politician is using his rhetoric in order to manipulate the masses. The bodies here play a crucial role in the dispersion power since the capacity of the body is not to be neglected:

> A body can possess various properties, and exist in various states. Bodies can be bearded or bald, naked or clothed, sweaty or dry, clean or dirty, healthy or diseased, alive or dead. Bodies can breathe and talk, see and hear, walk and grasp, gobble and chew, swallow and digest, suckle and suck, masticate and ejaculate, excrete and procreate. (Filling 2009)

The most important aspect of the body that is necessary in order to render *Coriolanus* is the one that Filling calls "organic" conception of the body (ibid). The mobs on the streets of Rome are people with needs:

> (...) persons with bodily needs, needs that are not satisfied in a dearth crisis. Fundamentally, from their point of view, the citizens are neither rebel members, nor dissatisfied members of the body politic, but dissatisfied bodies, bodies dissatisfied with the commonwealth, who will not be fed empty tales anymore. There is a genuine political crisis in this initial scene of *Coriolanus*. (Borot 2007)

So conceived, a body is an organism which organizes or differentiates itself into different organs or members, each organ performing a specialized function essential to the perpetuation and maintenance of the whole. (Filling 2009)

In the introduction to this section a great effort was made to tie the two plays/adaptations on the account of their excessive bloodiness – for both Coriolanus and Macbeth are frequently depicted as being covered in blood and, just like the worlds that they inhabit, they are bloody. Blood cannot be washed off hands, faces or daggers. *Macbeth* begins and ends with slaughter. There is more and more blood, everyone walks in it; it floods the stage. Kott (1964: 90) The metaphor of the bleeding body is something that is in common to both *Macbeth* and *Coriolanus* and this imagery of the bleeding body is the key aspect of how body politics imbues the plays; the excess of blood in both plays signifies violence that is being done to the body. *Macbeth* is a famously violent play. Interestingly, most of the killings take place offstage, but throughout the play the characters provide the audience with gory descriptions of the carnage, from the opening scene where the captain describes Macbeth and Banquo wading in blood on the battlefield, to the endless references to the bloodstained hands of Macbeth and his wife. The action is ended by a pair of bloody battles: in the first, Macbeth defeats the invaders; in the second, he is slain and beheaded by Macduff. In between is a series of murders: Duncan, Duncan's chamberlains, Banquo, Lady Macduff, and Macduff's son all come to bloody ends. By the end of the action, blood seems to be everywhere.

Indeed, blood is everywhere in *Macbeth,* beginning with the opening battle between the Scots and the Norwegian invaders, which is described in harrowing terms by the wounded captain in Act 1, scene 2. Once Macbeth and Lady Macbeth embark upon their murderous journey, blood comes to symbolize their guilt, and they begin to feel that their crimes have stained them in a way that cannot be washed clean. "Will all great Neptune's ocean wash this blood / Clean from my hand?" Macbeth cries after he has killed Duncan, even as his wife scolds him and says that a little water will do the job (II, 2). Later, though, she comes to share his horrified sense of being stained: "Out, damned spot; out, I say . . . who would have thought the old man to have had so much blood in him?" she asks as she wanders through the halls of their castle near the close of the play (V, 1). Blood symbolizes the guilt that sits like a permanent stain on the consciences of both Macbeth and Lady Macbeth, one that hounds them to their graves.

While the imagery representing body politics in *Macbeth* is connected to blood, in *Coriolanus* it is closely tied to the body which is a site of conflict; a class conflict, between the political and economic elite, or patricians, and the poorer but more numerous plebeians. The plebeians as they appear in this drama have no ideal of their own to set up, but are defaulters to the conception of duty recognized by all.

They "cannot rule, nor ever will be ruled (I, 3) "; their "affections are a sick man's appetite, who desires most that which would increase his evil (ibid)." This is the very point of the famous Fable of the Belly and Members, with which Menenius strikes the key-note of the whole play. The belly and the members are not coordinate limbs of the body; the drift of the parable is that the belly is the state, and the members, so far as they are not serving the belly, are disturbers of the general health of the physical or political body. For both patricians and plebeians there is but one ideal, that of service to the state; and to this ideal the patrician party is wholly devoted. It is true that at one excited point of the conflict a representative of the plebeians - as if with a sudden insight into the thought of future ages (one might say of our ages) – cries out (III;1): "What is the city but the people?"

To answer this question one must take notice that the universe of Shakespeare's *Coriolanus* is limited to the mud, bricks and mortar of Rome. (Moulton 2011). In Fiennes' modern movie adaptation this depiction is also visible:

Rome is the defining entity in the lives of all its citizens. Their spiritual atmosphere is the air of Rome, their mental horizons end at the walls of Rome, and their lives end under the soil of Rome. They are born in Rome, they are then shaped by Rome, so that they may serve Rome. They are even to die for Rome, and Rome will then remember them. Rome is their cradle, their world, their grave, and their monument. (ibid)

The recent expulsion of Rome's kings has created a power vacuum, and the two classes now fight over whether elite opinion or the popular will should hold sway in the Roman polity. There is however, a sense of a vacuum in Shakespeare's Rome (Hornaday 2012) and this vacuum is what Fiennes also depicts in his version of the play. It is the attempt to fill this vacuum that the politicians like Menenius are trying to fill. The main question that Fiennes' adaptation poses is – whether or not is Coriolanus able to fill this vacuum. As a number of critics have pointed out, these same issues of class conflict and the question of oligarchic vs. popular rule similarly plagued Shakespeare's own time, as tensions rose between King James and the English Parliament. However, the playwright veils his own point of view on such issues with deliberate ambiguity. On the one hand, Coriolanus' expulsion seems to be a clear warning about the dangerous volatility of the popular will; the plebeians quickly bend under the tribunes' manipulation instead of considering Coriolanus' service to his country. However, while his exile seems unjust, Coriolanus remains manifestly unsuited for the consulship, in both character and temperament; his angry contempt for the plebeians seems to stem less from political principle than from self-interest and pride. Thus, the play vividly presents political issues while refraining from taking sides.

Shakespeare uses nature imagery and the presence of blood as mediums for explaining the parallels between characters, their actions, and the nature of fate that is something that both Macbeth and Coriolanus fail to change. The weight of Macbeth and Lady Macbeth's crimes are represented through the reaction of nature to those actions. Shakespeare shows this relationship by using body politic. Body politic may states that if politics go wrong, then nature goes wrong. In Macbeth, the murder of King Duncan is the political flaw, where chaos is nature's reaction. The first example of body politics occurs when Duncan arrives at Macbeth's castle. 'This guest of summer, / the temple-haunting martlet does approve, / . . . that the heaven's breath / Smells wooingly here; (I, 4). The irony of a church bird dwelling on a house of evil shows that something is wrong in nature. On the night of the murder, Lady Macbeth says, 'I heard the owl scream and the crickets cry' (II, 2). Her statement is a revelation to the audience, because owls give a pleasant, calming 'hoot and a cricket's voice is not that of a cry, but that of a sweet 'chirp'. In scene four Ross wonders at, '. . . the heaven, as troubled with man's act, / . . . By 'th clock 'tis day, / and yet the dark lamp strangles the traveling lamp' (II, 4). Ross in this scene speculates as to why the heavens are troubled because there is an eclipse in the sky. In other words, it is day, but yet darkness reigns. It is therefore quite fitting that on the night of Duncan's murder, there is an eclipse. The fact that an eclipse is rare also supports the possibility that something is wrong in nature:

> The supernatural world is the most extreme example of power that is beyond human control, and it is therefore an apt symbol for the unpredictable forces of human motivation. This larger aspect of evil influences our impression of its more particular manifestation in the man Macbeth. Thus, the pervasive magic in

the world of *Macbeth* supports our awareness that the behavior of the protagonist is, in human terms, unnatural. (Boyce 2005: 350)

As in other Shakespearean tragedies, Macbeth's grotesque murder spree is accompanied by a number of unnatural occurrences in the natural realm. From the thunder and lightning that accompany the witches' appearances to the terrible storms that rage on the night of Duncan's murder, these violations of the natural order reflect corruption in the moral and political orders. In the play Macbeth is labeled a 'tyrant' by other lords at his court, who hope that his deposition would 'Give to our tables' meat, sleep to our nights, / Free from our feasts and banquets bloody knives' (III, 6). Lennox, noble lord concurs with the others, describing Scotland as 'our suffering country' (ibid). This discussion of Scotland's suffering suggests that Macbeth is an unsuccessful ruler when judged according to the body politic model, since he cannot act for the good of the realm of Scotland. In the adaptation, likewise, Macbeth is shown to be a good chef, but he fails to make good rapport with the customers like Duncan does. Upon usurping the throne, Macbeth brings only chaos to Scotland— symbolized in the bad weather and bizarre supernatural events—and offers no real justice, only a habit of capriciously murdering those he sees as a threat. As the embodiment of tyranny, he must be overcome by Malcolm so that Scotland can have a true king once more. The tragedy of Macbeth—with its bloody portrait of a "disjoint[ed]" universe where the stability of the body politic is invalidated by the reign of an illegitimate tyrant—fully pertains to the antique figural tradition of bodily political metaphors (Spicci 2007). Macbeth's usurpation of Duncan transcends the politics of the kingdom, and threatens a natural good deeply embedded in Macbeth (Bloom 1998: 521) – so Macbeth is a battlefield in himself does he fight an ultimate battle that is finally won by evil.

Of all Shakespeare's plays, *Macbeth* is most "a tragedy of blood", not just in its murders but in the ultimate implications of Macbeth's imagination being itself bloody. The usurper Macbeth moves in a consistent phantasmagoria of blood: blood is the prime constituent of his imagination. He *sees* that what opposes him is blood in one aspect – call it nature in the sense that he opposes nature – and that this opposing force thrusts him into shedding more blood. "It will have blood, they say, blood will have blood". (Bloom 1998: 520-521). Moreover, when juxtaposing the spectacle of the 'bleeding country' with the concrete vision of the 'tyrant's head' (IV, 3) one cam clearly see the link to Menenius' fable of the belly displayed in *Coriolanus.*

The 'fable of the belly' can be linked to 'digestion' so as to justify the adoption of a medical hermeneutical perspective, it is likewise true that the numerous references to the semantic areas of "eating" and "drinking' (Spicci 2007). This casts a new light on the play's pathological dimension. In fact the progressive accumulation of images of difficult, eve 'unnatural', digestive processes actually makes it possible for the body politic in *Macbeth* to be transformed into a huge, sickly body in want of medical care (ibid). Now Shakespeare's dramatic experiment reveals its darkest sinews: first, he adopts one of the most influential metaphors of society as the main ideological scaffolding of his play; then he moulds it by making constant reference to Renaissance physiology, so as to exploit the figurative potential emerging from the combination of the body politic theory and human physiology; last, he leads the audience to recognize that the functioning of the State is more than simply similar to that of the human body. In *Macbeth*, the State is a real human body. Therefore, bodily dismemberment, which follows what has been an authentically exorcising evacuation, coincides with Macbeth's physical death, and the horrific vision of Macbeth's severed head testifies that political liberation is the ultimate result of a terrible, yet real, surgical operation. Once 'purged', the body politic can start functioning again; its organs can secrete and absorb vital bodily liquids, and blood can irrigate its limbs. The foreign body has been removed from the congested body politic. Now 'the time is free' (V, 9), but political surgery has been fatally inaugurated with the death of Macbeth. Mark Brozel makes the image of dying Macbeth especially vulnerable so as to exploit the visual performance of a dying body. However, this decay of the body on a micro-level is best seen on another example and that is Lady Macbeth. Both the plays as well as the adaptation offer a decaying image of Lady Macbeth when she falls in a state of madness. Here, symbolically her body betrays *her* and, ultimately, it leads her and her husband to their deaths. Joanna Levin has written that Lady Macbeth represents the entire spectrum of unnatural womanhood within the early modern world (Preston Leonard 2009: 70). Lady Macbeth is an amalgam of the disorderly, chaos-inducing individual. She was given epithets of a witch as she plots killings and invokes evil spirits. Marjorie

Garber claims, the disintegration of Lady Macbeth is even more disturbing than that of Macbeth himself since it is so sudden and more complete (Preston Leonard 2009:70). Foucault writes of Lady Macbeth as one in the long line of early modern and Shakespearian truth-seekers "driven mad not because of evil urgings to Macbeth but because of her later recognition of the further consequences and actions taken by her prior ruthlessness" (Preston Leonard 2009:70-71):

To the moral world belongs also *the madness of just punishment*, which chastises, along with the disorders of the mind, those of the heart. But it has still other powers: the punishment it inflicts multiplies by nature insofar as, by punishing itself, it unveils the truth. The justification of this madness is that it is truthful. Truthful since the sufferer already experiences, in the vain whirlwind of hallucinations, what will for all the eternity be the pain of his punishment... Truthful, too, because the crime hidden from all eyes dawns like day in the night of this strange punishment; madness, in its wild untamable words, proclaims its own meaning; in its chimeras, it utters its secret truth: it cries speak for its conscience. Thus Lady Macbeth's delirium reveals to those who "have known what they should know", words long uttered only to "dead pillows". (Preston Leonard 2009:70-71.)

This is not merely a body politics-related issue but more generally and, in cultural materialist context of our time, a reminder that there is no security in our bodies' just like, for that matter, there is no security in literature. The harrowing image of the decay of Lady Macbeth's mind is surely amongst the most potent in all of Shakespeare and, most definitely, evidence of how body politics operates on a micro-level, for the fight takes place in the body, not just around it.

Coriolanus too serves as a battleground for even the fiercest warrior in all of Shakespeare is not spared of body politics. Coriolanus, though no fool, is primarily a warrior, a man of action little given to inward retrospection. He is a man completely lacking in political gifts - a stubborn soldier, brought down by an overweening pride and an inability to compromise with the forces that seek his downfall:

A representative of the patrician class of Rome, Coriolanus' prowess in battle would seem to make him an ideal hero for the masses; however, he utterly lacks the common touch, and his fear of popular rule allows him to be construed as an enemy of the people... Thus, his fate of exile is appropriate; he truly has no place in the new political life of his city. (Moulton 2011)

Though Coriolanus is himself unsubtle, preferring to express himself directly (indeed, this contributes to his downfall), he is surrounded by craftier, more manipulative characters. His close friend, Menenius, serves as the perfect foil in this regard; for though he shares Coriolanus's aristocratic sensibilities and suspicion of the plebeian class, Menenius's smooth tongue and talent for compromise enable him to skate through the difficulties that are imposed on Coriolanus. Menenius's counterparts on the plebeian side are the two tribunes,

Sicinius and Brutus, whose talent for demagoguery and manipulation of the masses enable them to turn the people of Rome against Coriolanus – an easy task, given the hero's appetite for violent outbursts. The play's eponymous hero therefore is a difficult man with whom to sympathize.

But *Coriolanus* is much more than that. Coriolanus is *constrained* (Middleton 2012). In *Coriolanus* we have a story of a downfall of a "too absolute" leader. (ibid). Fiennes' adaptation, then hinges on the very character of Coriolanus. "Coriolanus" is a bloody but brilliant contemporary depiction of war, political manipulation and the prejudices of opposing social extremes. Wars, politics and angry demonstrators (not out of place in Europe) unravel and expose the inner nature of Coriolanus. In this regard, one might claim that that "Coriolanus" is a reflection of how warriors make poor political leaders, or how a person cannot be made to fit an office. In the film we only glimpse that Shakespeare's drama is also about the struggle between the plebeians and the aristocracy. The allegory of the human frame and the state, more notable more for its politics than for poetry, is omitted. But it is a key to the plot. There is indeed little poetry and all that remaining prose is directed towards the manipulation of the masses. They are ever so frequently manipulated against Coriolanus by the two unscrupulous Tribunes, Brutus and Sicinius. One minute they are full of his praise, the next, the fickle crowd yells for his death. It soon becomes clear in *Coriolanus* that the body politic has broken down, and neither the patricians nor the plebeians are wholly innocent or wholly at fault. If the plebeians are rebellious, the patricians are neglecting their duty to take care of and nourish the plebeians. The

First Citizen emphasizes this in his speech in act one: "Care for us? They ne'er cared for us yet. Suffer us to famish, and their storehouses crammed with grain." On the individual level, Coriolanus' pride and disdain for the plebeians cuts him off from them in a manner that is destructive to both sides. This breakdown in the relationship between patricians and plebeians is as dangerous to the health of society as a breakdown in the relationship between belly and body parts would be to the health of a person. In addition, Shakespeare suggests through imagery that the plebeians, without strong governance from the patricians, are incomplete men, like body parts separated from the whole organism. Menenius calls the First Citizen "the great toe of this assembly" (I. 1).

Another variant on the metaphor of the body politic that Coriolanus shares with Macbeth is that of the diseased body. Coriolanus refers to the mob as a disease, "measles" (III. 1). When they express their discontent, he says they are "rubbing the poor itch of [their] opinion" so that they "Make [themselves] scabs" (I.1) Their desires, he says, are "A sick man's appetite, who desires most that / Which would increase his evil" (ibid). Typically of this ambivalent play, however,the metaphor of the unhealthy body is also used against Coriolanus. Sicinius calls Coriolanus "a disease that must be cut away" (ibid) and refers to his mind as "a poison" (ibid). Brutus dismisses Menenius's insistence on peaceful and legal processes to try Coriolanus as "cold ways" that "are very poisonous / Where the disease is violent" (ibid). This is a reference to the Renaissance doctrine of "humors" or bodily fluids, where disease was seen as an excess of hot or cold humors, and medicines that were hot or cold in nature were prescribed to cure it. In *Macbeth* there are numerous comparisons with the diseased body of Scotland. The symbolic imagery of politics that is in the core of *Macbeth* allows us to see what happens when Macbeth transforms it into a huge, sickly body in want of medical care (Spicci 2007) and this allows us to see that Macbeth, like Coriolanus, although being a great warrior, brings his country ruin and destruction. Macbeth's and Coriolanus' virtues include their military prowess and their sense of honor. Convinced that humility and compromise clash with his own nature, Coriolanus simply cannot make the gestures necessary to win the plebeians' respect, and his inability to control his unruly tongue only facilitates his adversaries' plans to bring him down. Ultimately, his chief fault is childishness, a failing reflected in his submissiveness to his mother, Volumnia. It is her ambition and bloodlust, more than anything else, that have shaped his character. Perhaps Shakespeare's most overtly political plays, more so even than the histories, *Coriolanus* and *Macbeth* alike take as its heroes men completely lacking in political gifts - a stubborn soldier, brought down by an overweening pride and an inability to compromise with the forces that seek his downfall and an ambitious warlord that cannot satisfy his appetite for power. A representative of the patrician class of Rome, Coriolanus' prowess in battle would seem to make him an ideal hero for the masses; however, he utterly lacks the common touch, and his fear of popular rule allows him to be construed as an enemy of the people. Macbeth's bloody reign has a fearsome similarity with the end of *Coriolanus* wherein Ralph Fiennes' character realizes that he has brought doom to the only thing that ever meant to him – Rome. The issues of power, politics, culture and economy as displayed in this section are intertwined so as to echo in our contemporary world.

The issues that both Brozel's and Fiennes' adaptations address are fresh and politically up-to-date. Their contemporariness in the relation of power and the problematizing of the issue of body politics makes them relevant to the audience of the 21st century. A remnant of this problematizing is perhaps best captured in Brozel's adaptation. Warning Macbeth to beware Macduff, the three bin men are throwing bags of waste into the back of their truck in the alley by the restaurant. As they speak to Macbeth, the three enigmatic men are letting him know that they know the entire story:

> MACBETH How – how do you know these things?
> BIN MAN 1 The whole story is here. From flaunted sperm in banana-flavored rubber, right
> through to the yellow hacked-out gob of ancient drunks. All of life.
> BIN MAN 2 And the special brew.
> BIN MAN 3 Dipping needles.
> BIN MAN1 All the great excitements that get us from the cradle to the grave. The sound and the fury.
> BIN MAN 2 It all ends with us.
> BIN MAN 3 Incinerated.
> BIN MAN 2 Obliterated.
> BIN MAN 1 No more.
> BIN MAN 2 Yesterday's breakfast, yesterday's meat, yesterday's men.
> BIN MAN 3 All your yesterdays.
> BIN MAN 2 All our tomorrows
> ALL (driving away) Bye bye, bye bye, bye bye…

This incredibly rich and potent fragment from the adaptation if filled with some of the classic *Macbeth* quotations ('The sound and the fury'; Tomorrow and tomorrow') serving as a sort of an homage to the play. However, when observed more closely we can see some remnants of the body politics. The body taken as a visceral image of representation for 'yesterday' and 'tomorrow' are merged into a sole vision of bodily emissions (Kidnie 2009: 118) – the 'flaunted' sperm and the 'hacked-out' expectorate - as discarded human waste. Everything begins and ends with the disposal of meat and men (ibid). Shakespeare was professionally fascinated too by the comportment of men and women facing the end" (Greenblatt 2004: 276) His most famous lines on the subject come from *Macbeth*, in the description of the last moments in the life of a thane who had betrayed his king:

> Nothing in his life
> Became him like the leaving it. He died
> As one that has been studied in his death
> To throw away the dearest thing he owed
> As 'twere a careless trifle
> (*Macbeth* I, 4)

The flawed characters of Coriolanus and Macbeth are indeed, as the title of the chapter suggests, men against fate, both doomed to challenge their destiny and in doing so destined to fall. Their fall from grace is something that the modern man can relate to because at the core of both of the tragic protagonists lie men stripped of their battle prowess and made bare; they bring the battle from the battlefields onto their consciousness and thus make *themselves* warriors *and* battlefields alike. This brings modernity to Fiennes' adaptation for Coriolanus, very much like Macbeth, is hero as trapped between two worlds – he is a kingly figure, born to command; yet, at the same time he finds himself inhabiting a republican political reality that – though he himself has helped to create it--he cannot endure. Thus, his fate of exile is appropriate; like Macbeth he truly has no place in the new political life of his city. Coriolanus and Macbeth alike embody two figures of modernity: the individual who follows his individual judgment, even in the face of obvious error and failure, on the one hand, and on the other, the illegitimate ruler who, though he rose to power following legitimate rules, becomes a tyrant by the way he rules. Caius Martius Coriolanus and Macbeth thus become types of modern men, or men of emerging modernity.

Coriolanus and Macbeth: Men of Emerging Modernity

David Haglund writing for *Slate* questions T.S. Eliot's claim that *Coriolanus* and not *Hamlet* is Shakespeare's greatest tragedy:

> In 1919, T.S. Eliot published an essay that elevates literary contrarianism to heights that have rarely been equaled. The central argument of "Hamlet and His Problems," which first appeared in the *Athenaeum* and was later collected in *The Sacred Wood*, is that *Hamlet* is inferior to *Coriolanus*. Eliot goes on to insist that the Bard's greatest tragedy is actually a play few people paid much attention to then or now: *Coriolanus*, just adapted for the screen by Ralph Fiennes. (Haglund 2012)

Eliot's notion that *Coriolanus* is Shakespeare's best play, even superior to *Hamlet*, because it makes more sense is brought to the foreground with Fiennes' adaptation of *Coriolanus* (ibid). The near century that has passed since Eliot's essay and now we have

Fiennes' movie to show why this play has intrigued great critics like Eliot. The modern *Coriolanus* in Fiennes' hands quite sagely turns into the issues of our world today. Fiennes manages to achieve this with ease and uncanny relevance (Hornaday 2012):

> Scenes of an angry mob of "plebeians" organizing, rioting, and using the media to spread the grievances against the aristocratic "1 percent" has obvious parallels to Wall Street and today's global economic discontent. Other scenes of urban warfare—bodies in the street and bombed-out cars—evoke contemporary war zones like Iraq. But there are also timely commentaries on the role of personality in politics, the way that handlers can manipulate a politician's image, and the speed with which public opinion can turn on a candidate when the slightest gaffe is recorded and virally spread throughout the populace. (Haglund 2012)

Fiennes has managed to make of *Coriolanus* a study of political rhetoric as timely and urgent as anything on cable news ticker (Hornaday 2012). And indeed the movie is as timely as it can only be – the impeccable attention that Fiennes gives to mass-culture details, from the narrative exposition delivered by a BBC–esque news anchor (ibid), the movie's opening sequence with the political demonstration of the Roman citizens or the modern TV debate wherein Coriolanus participates in order to secure his consulship. In such a modern setting not even the original Shakespearian language seems archaic when spoken by people wearing modern military fatigues or when delivered by the way of Skype. Rather, it flickers with dynamics, freshness but also with urgency. The existing news footages of chaotic crushes outside Serbian parliament are inserted into the movie; there are footages of tanks on the move; of displeased citizens protesting against the Milošević regime and all is combined to send a political media – saturated message. One could argue that Eliot indeed had a point when claiming that *Coriolanus* was not given enough attention (Haglund 2012) and that it bears relevance today perhaps more than ever. Several renowned critics, including Slavoj Žižek agree:

> Fiennes filmed his adaptation in Belgrade—a stroke of genius according to Slovenian philosopher Žižek. In Žižek's interpretation, Fiennes has re-imagined the rebellious army of the play as "leftist guerilla rebels," and has transformed Coriolanus from "a fanatical anti-democrat" into a "figure of the radical left." Fiennes and Logan, Žižek says, have "done the impossible, confirming in the process T.S. Eliot's claim that *Coriolanus* is superior to *Hamlet*."

When one sees this impact of *Coriolanus*, one might wonder what kind of political parallels are entailed in this, seemingly shallow and unpopular play. Here are the parallels that were connected to the play throughout the centuries. :

For Shakespeare's original audiences in around 1608, the clamour of the people and the threats to the state might have evoked recent memories of the Gunpowder Plot. Coriolanus himself, a haughty warrior who betrays his country, would have found ready models in the Earl of Essex, who had risen up against Elizabeth I at the end of her reign, or Sir Walter Raleigh, in the middle of his long imprisonment in the Tower of London, on a charge of treason. In the

18th century, adapters rewrote the play to remove the ambivalences in Coriolanus' character and made it clear that virtue would be rewarded and vice punished. Victorian productions emphasised the nobility of Coriolanus and made the mob "dirty swine". In 1910, a reviewer of a Stratford-upon-Avon production noticed "the peculiar appositeness" of a new version, at a time "when a social upheaval or struggle is taking place between the aristocracy and democracy". In the 1980s, British productions drew parallels with Thatcherite politics and the Falklands war, while Americans compared Coriolanus with Lieutenant-Colonel Oliver North, the flawed Vietnam veteran at the centre of the Iran-Contra affair in 1986. When audiences in 2012 watch an uprising of the people, we cannot but think of last year's Arab Spring. The Roman mob that Fiennes films in Belgrade seems to echo the potent fury of the crowds in Tahrir Square. When Coriolanus defies the citizens, the more sinister responses of the Assad regime in Syria are brought to mind. (Horspool 2012).

We see that when Ralph Fiennes picked modern-day Serbia as the setting for his big-screen adaptation of Shakespeare's *Coriolanus*, the parallels were obvious – among others recalling the Balkan conflicts of the 1990s. Dragan Mićanović, who plays Titus Lartius, a comrade of Coriolanus, reveals in an interview:

> If we learn any lessons from Coriolanus, it's that the circle of violence will never end unless we make a full stop (…) And if politicians are only out to serve themselves rather than the people, whole nations will suffer. I have felt that very strongly in

my country. I grew up in a house near the Bosnia-Herzegovina border that has been in five different countries over the decades. That's the ridiculous modern history of my nation: I live in a country that has suffered so much and is still suffering because of terrible political decisions (Hall 2012)

The modern history of the Balkans that Mićanović describes in his interview is indeed one that has suffered a great deal because of the political decisions that severely harmed the population of former Yugoslavia. In this regard Fiennes' rendition of *Coriolanus* stresses the state in Serbia that still carries the seal of the 1990s war as Mićanović continues to reveal the interview:

> After 400 years, we still have Coriolanuses in the world," he says. "You see guys walking around Belgrade with the faces of war criminals such as Radovan Karadzic and Ratko Mladic on their T-shirts. They are still national heroes to some people. (...) Mladic was a soldier, and now he's in prison. If he read Coriolanus he could find his story in it (...) Even though the war was over, the Serb president Slobodan Milosevic was still in power. It was a terrible time and I couldn't live there any more. He just didn't care at all about culture, so we could do what we wanted – and we did some fantastic anti-government plays that told exactly what was going on in the Balkans. (Hall 2012)

Fiennes' *Coriolanus* is the final word of the plays that comment on the Balkan atrocities. With the horrific conflicts in the Balkans still a comparatively recent memory; such re-enactments could have been an uncomfortable reminder. (Horspool 2012). Coriolanus' message is far more powerful, though, than a simple modern war film. Mićanović hopes his fellow Serbians will recognize that: "When Serbians see Belgrade as Ancient Rome and how, because of corrupt politics, heroes become villains, I hope it will change their minds of how things should be. But I'm not sure. We learn so little from our mistakes". (Hall 2012)

There is no dispute that *Macbeth* is a play more popular than *Coriolanus*. However, *Macbeth was* always considered by actors to be an unlucky play. Many will refuse to even mention the play's name. They call it, instead, 'The Scottish play'. This popular trivia fact about one of Shakespeare's greatest tragedies was aptly incorporated into the 2005 BBC's *Shakespeare Retold* series directed by Mark Brozel. In BBC's *Macbeth* we have Joe Macbeth, a popular chef who, in his kitchen, forbids naming the celebrity chef Gordon Ramsey. It is as if the name of Gordon Ramsey and *Macbeth* were names of something holy and uncanny. Similarly to the superstitious actors, the equally superstitious cooks do not name Ramsey by name, but they call him 'The Scottish Chef'. It is a wonderfully apt way of addressing a cultural phenomenon such as celebrity chefs, which have taken over the British TV screens with their shows and introduced the British cuisine anew with the likes of Gordon Ramsey and Jamie Oliver, and taking these celebrity chefs and equating them with the superstitious and uncanny influence of *Macbeth*.

Just like *Macbeth* the play begins with witches, so too does the adaptation begin with bin men. The equating of witches with bin men could be strange at first glance, but one must bear in mind that the image of witches depicted across the fairy tales and, indeed in Shakespeare, has always been used to represent marginalized groups of people such as women. This instance might be appropriated in our contemporary socio-cultural context by casting the economically marginalized group of bin men as taking the undesirable role of the witches. Just like the witches who bring the prophecy to thane Macbeth that he will be king, so do the bin men bring word to the chef Joe Macbeth that the restaurant will belong to him. Marjorie Garber in her book *Shakespeare After Shakespeare* (2004: 697) claims that the witches from *Macbeth* are not merely mythological beings, but that, when on stage, they a persuasive psychological reality of their own. Indeed, the psychological presence of the bin men just like the witches is full of omens that allude to the ensuing action throughout the film: 'We know everything, we're bin men. There's nothing we don't know' – this sentence evokes the weird sisters from the play and their prophetic vision of Macbeth's reign. One might, as Harold Bloom does, why are we unable to resist identifying with Macbeth. In Bloom's words, Macbeth so dominates his play that we have nowhere else to turn. (Bloom 1998: 517). In identifying with him we can perhaps see how blind ambition leads to an ultimate downfall and that, indeed, "Blood will have blood" – for in a tragedy, like in life, all is pre-destined.

Coriolanus is much more difficult to identify with, for he is one of the most hateful characters, and quite possibly the most hateful protagonist, in the whole of world of Shakespeare. His only virtues are the military ones. He hates *everybody* else in the play (and, one strongly suspects, himself), even the two he also loves—his opposite number the Volscian general Aufidius and his mother Volumnia, the only woman in Shakespeare who can match the strong-willed Lady Macbeth. The rest—the rank-and-file Volscian enemy, the Roman rabble, the Roman senate—he hates without mitigation, and virtually every word out of his mouth expresses his contempt for them. This makes a film of *Coriolanus* an improbable proposition; Ralph Fiennes's new version would seem to be the first that isn't based on a previous stage production which is the reason behind why Fiennes' film is a triumph; not only an exciting film that draws new audiences to this difficult play, but a rare re-imagining that isn't just a translation of a stage production.

Coriolanus in not only a powerful tragedy but also a constant ideological temptation for directors (Garber 2009:62): perhaps no other play of Shakespeare has been so appropriated across the political spectrum: Laurence Olivier memorably played the role of Coriolanus in two productions. However it was in Germany of the first half of the twentieth century that *Coriolanus* gained popularity and this coincided with some extraordinary developments in theater as well as in politics (ibid). This play was a favorite during the period of National Socialism in Germany because it seemed to stress the status of a singular charismatic leader (Garber 2009:63). The character of Coriolanus would become politicized to the extent of being offered as an admirable example, "as Adolf Hitler wishing to lead his beloved German fatherland" (ibid). The hero, Coriolanus, as Bloom called him the

113

greatest killing machine in all Shakespeare (Bloom 1998: 577) is a loner (Christ 2002:264). He is used to act alone, unable to establish ordinary human relationships: "He is a site of conflicting human qualities: courage and arrogance, strength and weakness, angry independence o others and an almost- childish dependency of his mother, Volumnia" (ibid). When we come to look at Shakespeare's *Coriolanus* we can see scene by scene in which in which the thematic of estrangement, distancing, defamiliorization and alienation are performed in a context of a performance-within-a-performance. Marjorie Garber in her book *Shakespeare and Modern Culture* (2009) lists some examples:

- Martius's astonishment at his mother Volumnia's instruction that he falsify himself in front of the common people in order to gain their votes for the consulate.
- His angry rejection of Rome ("I banish *you*") when popular favors turn against him.
- His rapprochement with the enemy general, Aufidius, formerly his foe.
- His expectation that the people of the vanquished city of Corioles would accept without ambivalence his honorific surname, "Coriolanus" (the man who defeated Corioles)
- His willed isolation from family and friends and his ardent wish for self-invention ("as if a man were author of himself / and had no other kin).
- His refusal to admit entreaties on a personal level when the Roman general Cominius seeks his aid ("He was kind of nothing, titleless").

- His ultimate stripping or unmasking by the crafty Aufidius, who removes, one by one, the names by which he has been known (Corolanus, Martius), leaving him only with the insulting "boy", a word he repeats over and over in disbelief. (Garber 2009: 66-67).

The eponymous hero Coriolanus is a difficult man with whom to sympathize. His virtues include his military prowess (amply displayed in the play's battle scenes) and his sense of honor--but his honor easily lapses into unpleasant pigheadedness. Among his primary enemies lurk two clever schemers, Brutus and Sicinius, but, as Coriolanus is incapable of scheming himself, he is at a disadvantage from the beginning. Yet the two tribunes are hardly Edmunds or Iagos; Coriolanus' difficulties are less their fault than the fault of his own stubbornness and lack of self-control. Convinced that humility and compromise clash with his own nature, he simply cannot make the gestures necessary to win the plebeians' respect, and his inability to control his unruly tongue only facilitates his adversaries' plans to bring him down. Ultimately, his chief fault is childishness, a failing reflected in his submissiveness to his mother, Volumnia. It is her ambition and bloodlust, more than anything else, that have shaped his character:

Like Othello and Macbeth, Coriolanus is a successful warrior who finds himself in situation— here, the political world of Rome—to which he is temperamentally unsuited and in which he can be manipulated by others. Politically unsophisticated and emotionally immature, he can neither strike political deals with the tribunes nor resist his mother's insistence that he do so. He is reduced to blind vengeance, but she blocks him in that direction as well. Under these pressures, his great strength can only destroy him. His fate contains the irony found in all Shakespeare's tragedies: With greatness comes great weakness. Coriolanus's pride makes him great, but it also brings about his downfall. (Boyce 2005: 87)

Both Macbeth and Coriolanus have within their consciousness a spark of the humane that is, as some critics has noticed, terrifying to identify with. "I think we most identify with Macbeth because we also have the sense that we are violating our own natures; as he does his" (Bloom 1998: 534). Though Macbeth is a brave general and a powerful lord, his wife is far from subordinate to his will. Indeed, she often seems to control him, either by crafty manipulation or by direct order. And it is Lady Macbeth's deep-seated ambition, rather than her husband's, that ultimately propels the plot of the play by goading Macbeth to murder Duncan. Macbeth does not need any help coming up with the idea of murdering Duncan, but it seems unlikely that he would have committed the murder without his wife's powerful taunts and persuasions. Brozel's production is in this aspect close to "the productions regarding the celebration of the female characters" (Bulman 1996: 200). The celebration of the equality of spouses in marriage (that Shakespeare himself had stressed in his play) is successfully preserved in Brozel's adaptation by making the marriage of the Macbeths the corner stone of the plot. The marriage of the Macbeths was not typical for the time when Shakespeare wrote the play, but the adaptation seems to have transcended this and made Joe and Ella Macbeth equal partners. This could not have been done had Shakespeare himself made the original Macbeths in the play as the types of emerging modernity. Macbeths' marriage, like the couple themselves, is atypical, particularly by the standards of its time. Yet despite their odd power dynamic, the two of them seem surprisingly attached to one another, particularly compared to other married couples in Shakespeare's plays, in which romantic felicity appears primarily during courtship and marriages tend to be troubled. Macbeth offers an exception to this rule, as Macbeth and his wife are partners in the truest sense of the word. Of course, the irony of their "happy" marriage is clear—they are united by their crimes, their mutual madness, and their mounting alienation from the rest of humanity:

> Since Macbeth speaks fully a third of the drama's lines, and Lady Macbeth's role is truncated, Shakespeare's design upon us is manifest. We are to journey inward to Macbeth's heart of darkness, and there we will find ourselves more truly and more strange, murderers in and of the spirit. (Bloom 1998: 517-518)

Brozel's adaptation is reflecting the conflicted nature of contemporary society towards the position of women. On the one hand, they are still dedicated followers in a man's world, still dressing to attract male attention, still killing with their looks. On the other hand, they are allowed their 'singular ambition' – women in contemporary society are assertive *and* attractive. (Preston Leonard 2009:73) However this all can seem quite different if the woman is close to the *throne* - in this case her assertiveness can be seen as threatening. Macbeth, in the words of Harold Bloom, has "an excess of blood and energy" (Bloom 1998: 520) and "he exceeds us, in energy and in torment, but he also represents us, and we discover him more vividly within us the more deeply we delve" (Bloom 1998: 545) More directly and terrifying than any than any other character in Shakespeare, Macbeth voices the thought that we are all actors improvising our roles in a play of unknown authorship (Bate 1997: 271)

What makes both Macbeth and Coriolanus modern and made so as to appear contemporary in the 21st century is that both of them are imbued with estrangement, distancing, defamiliorization and alienation. Both Coriolanus and Macbeth are men bigger than their respective plays and adaptations. This is something that was well captured by directors Ralph and Mark Brozel in their movies:

> Telling a story for a television show is a visual exercise, and *Macbeth* relies at (...) key moments on contrived filmic techniques to encode villainy, to signal hallucinations and to express intrusion into everyday life of the surreal world of the weird sisters (imagined here as three bin men) (Kidnie 2009: 116)

Similarly as Jonathan Bate in his book *The Genius of Shakespeare* proposes (1997: 278), when ones sees not only an icon of humankind's capacity to make a contract with evil (as Macbeth and his bride do), but one rather sees his own highest imaginings, in all their thrilling power, in all their darkness. This is the uncanny aspect that is felt in *Macbeth* and *Coriolanus* alike. *Coriolanus* seems like a deliberate departure in Shakespeare's corpus away from plays like *Hamlet, Othello, King Lear* and *Anthony and Cleopatra*. (Bloom 1998: 577) It is as if Shakespeare deliberately decided to make Coriolanus different than other great warriors like Othello, Hotspur, Mark Anthony or Henry V. Coriolanus, like Macbeth, has something within him that is more apt to the 21st century than for Renaissance. In his search for his place under the Sun Coriolanus attempts to make himself fit for office only to discover that he cannot succeed. The greatest tragedy of Coriolanus is that there is that there is absolutely no place for him in the world of the communal and the communal, whether among Volscians or Romans (Bloom 1998: 580). Fiennes magnificently manages to capture this in his cinematography from the perspective of our contemporary world. The cinematography and point of view return to the kinetic news report style of the opening, cutting back and forth between reality and TV: Coriolanus' "trial" takes place in a studio resembling *News night*; the real-life BBC presenter Jon Snow pops up every now and then; there is even a red band at the bottom of the screen. The Fidelis network of Coriolanus' Rome is plainly our BBC. And importantly, this isn't just a postmodern flourish on Fiennes' part. By taking us out of the action and underscoring that we are watching a spectacle, Fiennes finds a cinematic counterpart to the Alienation Effect—one whose familiarity from a thousand movies and TV shows makes it all the more effective. This brings depth to the experience of *Coriolanus* because it seems as if we know Coriolanus – as if he is one of us. Brozel too manages to use the uncanny in his adaptation so as to make Macbeth appear humane and modern:

> Macbeth uses specific language patterns that set him aside from the rest:

> As he slices and tears the pig's flesh from is head, he instills in the would-be chefs gathered around him the rules of butchery – 'respect' and 'no waste' that double as life lessons. In another long monologue, Macbeth remembers the complex sensory experience of eating roast sparrow, describing the sound and feel of crunching down on the bones as a sort of childhood epiphany. The deliberate artistry of this narrated memory implicitly links the sensuality of meat and the sensuality of words, food preparation and poetry emerging as analogous aesthetic forms. (Kidnie 2009: 117)

Through the language that Brozel uses in his adaptation, the character of Macbeth is brought closer to us. Even Coriolanus with his retained Shakespearian verse does not sound archaic while he gives orders to a trooper via Skype. This along with the political demonstrations, invoking of the body politics actually makes Fiennes' film the ultimate Shakespearian adaptation. In the introduction it was mentioned that among Shakespearian adaptations worldwide, the most successful ones were the ones that were removed from the Western stage. This was especially true in the case of *Macbeth* – in Akira Kurosawa'a *Throne of Blood* (1957). After the analysis of *Coriolanus* one might be sure that Fiennes' film will join Kurosawa's masterpiece. *Macbeth,* being more popular than *Coriolanus,* was adapted more frequently than Fiennes' film but the relocation that Brozel achieved in the BBC *Shakespeare Retold* series makes it so removed from the mainstream stage and screen alike that this adaptation retains its incredible potency in our modern time.

Both *Coriolanus* and *Macbeth* alike make us feel as if they are our contemporaries since both offer alternative, yet uncanny realities wherein we have characters with whom it is difficult to identify on the surface. However, when scratched beneath the surface and discovering the underlying layers of darkness, ambition and greed we may recoil in horror when we recognize our appetites embedded in Coriolanus and Macbeth. Their tragic battle against their pre-destined doom makes them sympathetic but not enough for us to feel empathy for them. Nevertheless when we witness their dark desires and cravings it is impossible not to recognize a tiny fraction of ourselves in the two greatest Shakespearian warmongers who, ruled by their low appetites lose the battle for their souls to fate. Their struggle against their fate indeed does make them primal, even mythological characters that are universal in one's consciousness.

The following chapter will analyze the remaining two Shakespearian adaptations – both released under the BBC *Shakespeare Retold* umbrella: *Much Ado About Nothing* (2005) directed by Brian Percival and *The Taming of the Shrew* (2005) directed by David Richards. Unlike the more gritty and raw adaptations of the tragedies adapted by Fiennes and Brozel, Percival's and Richard's adaptations problematize the issues of love, marriage, gender as well as the socio-political context which these elements are structured around. The cultural materialist practice will make good use of the relocation of the original plays into modern-day Britain. Since we no longer have the traditional Shakespearian characters as noblemen and noblewomen but rather as politicians (such as the shrewish Katherine, no longer a rich and spoiled girl but rather an MP in the Parliament of Britain) or news anchors (Beatrice's and Benedick's verbal arguments are well relocated into a news studio), we can clearly see how the roles of characters have gained a fresh retrospective on the issues of modern-day dating, relationships, marriage and gender issues. The two comedies, in adapting their plot and characters to the 21st century, become models of the modern romance comedy.

MUCH ADO ABOUT NOTHING AND THE TAMING OF THE SHREW: THE COMEDIES FOR THE 21ST CENTURY

This chapter draws on the two adaptations of Shakespeare's comedies BBC released under the *Shakespeare Retold* umbrella: *Much Ado About Nothing* (2005) directed by Brian Percival and *The Taming of the Shrew* (2005) directed by David Richards. Just like the previous chapter dealt with the common themes that the two tragedies of *Coriolanus* and *Macbeth* have in common so too do these two comedies have one trait in common. Just like *Coriolanus* and *Macbeth* feature two characters that share common traits, in the same fashion do *Much Ado About Nothing* and *The Taming of the Shrew* feature two pairs of characters that are very similar in their behavior and character: Beatrice and Benedick from *Much Ado* and Katherine and Petruchio from *The Taming of the Shrew.* Much has been done with Shakespeare's comedies featuring his two most famous couples. The comedies *Much Ado About Nothing* and *The Taming of the Shrew* have within them perhaps the most prominent romantic couples in all of Shakespeare (save for the tragic couples of Mark Anthony and Cleopatra from *Anthony and Cleopatra* and Romeo and Juliet from the same named play) for the pairs – Beatrice / Benedick and Katherine / Petruchio are indeed mentioned instantly by many theater goers when asked about memorable characters from Shakespeare's comedies.

Although considered comedies in their core, both *Much Ado About Nothing* and *The Taming of the Shrew* have underlying layers of rather serious and dark shades of concern with issues such as betrayal, fidelity, marriage, love, hate and relationships. This is the reason why, for instance *Much Ado About Nothing* was and still is considered a 'dark comedy' or 'a problem play' – because of these underlying issues within this play that are addressed beneath the play's surface. Similar in its problematizing of the relationships and marriage *The Taming of the Shrew* likewise was and still is considered one of the plays that comments on the gender issues such as male supremacy over women. Although imbued with a light thematic and often featuring rather silly and whimsical issues, these comedies actually comment more on the society than we would presume for underneath this masquerade of light and often verbose humor lie vestiges of anger, betrayal, doubt and despair. These aspects that *Much Ado* and *The Taming of the Shrew* have in common make them closer to the plays with similar themes such as *All's Well That Ends Well, Troilus and Cressida, Measure for Measure* or *The Merchant of Venice.* As in the world so too is with Shakespeare – there is no black and white but merely a gray area where comedy manages to co-exist with tragedy. However, the above mentioned plays *are* comedies for they are categorized as such because they feature the common element in all comedy – a happy ending. However, the epithets 'problem play' or 'dark comedy' were assigned them for a reason – they signify enough evidence that there is a bitter-sweet aftertaste to experiencing their comedic effect. Unlike other 'merry comedies' by Shakespeare such as *The Comedy of Errors, Love's Labor Lost, The Two Gentlemen of Verona, A Midsummer Night's Dream* or *The Merry Wives of Windsor,* these comedies feature a part within them that threatens to become tragedy at any given moment. In this regard *Much Ado About Nothing* and *The Taming of the Shrew,* with occasional glances at their sordid themes, could be considered to be close to the plays *As You Like It* and *Twelfth Night,* two of Shakespeare's greatest comedies which similarly feature a tragic events which in the course of the play reverse into a happy ending. With a glance at the dark and tragic events that imbue *Much Ado* and *The Taming of the Shrew* we could say that they are close to *Coriolanus* and *Macbeth* discussed in the previous chapter, for at least they threaten to provide half of the gloomy vision that *Coriolanus* and *Macbeth* alas deliver. This is not to say that comedy and tragedy are genres that mutually exclude one another. We can find comical situations in tragedies as likely as we can find dark and gloomy traces of hatred, resentment and despair in comedies. As Alenka Zupančič in her book *The Odd One In: On Comedy* remarks:

> Tragedy is not – at least since Shakespeare, and particularly (although not exclusively) with Shakespeare – a monolithic genre. In tragedies we can find perfectly comic sequences (passages, episodes) which do not transform tragedy into comedy (or into tragicomedy), but exists in their specificity without affecting the structure of the tragic genre. (Zupančič 2008: 173)

The structure of the tragic genre is consistent in both *Coriolanus* and *Macbeth* alike but the 'tragedies' of *Much Ado About Nothing* and *The Taming of the Shrew* contain the essence of the transformative power of tragedy into comedy which Zupančič mentions in her book. We have situations in both plays / adaptations which threaten to make both comedies into becoming tragedies, or at least tragicomedies. Indeed, the line between tragedy and comedy is sometimes a blur. The comic sequences within tragedies Zupančić observes are very difficult to pinpoint in *Coriolanus* since the play as well as Fiennes' adaptation are devoid of any comic relief because both the thematic of *Coriolanus* as well as it tragic protagonist are cloaked in blood and violence. This makes *Coriolanus* one of Shakespeare's rare plays (perhaps the only one) that do not provide any comic relief. However, there is a very famous comic sequence in *Macbeth* with the porter scene (*Macbeth* II, 3). In fact, just before the porter scene, we have the tragic hero Macbeth who, after killing Duncan and feeling instant guilt because of the shameless deed, says unto his wife: "To know my deed, 'twere best not to know myself". After hearing 'knocking within' he says ironically to his wife: "Wake Duncan with thy knocking. I would thou couldst". This ironic statement brings about at least some comic relief that is amplified later on in the next scene. After the bloody imagery and dark tone of the previous scene, the porter's comedy comes as a needed change of tone. In this scene the Porter hears knocking at the gate and imagines that he is the porter at the door to Hell. The porter's joke that the door of the castle is like hell's gate is ironic, given the cruel and bloody events that are taking place within the castle's walls. These kinds of utterances do not transform tragedy into comedy (or into tragicomedy for that matter), but they do exist independently without affecting the structure of the tragedy. The opposite occurs in *Much Ado* and *The Taming of the Shrew*. For example, many critics have noted that the plot of *Much Ado About Nothing* shares significant elements with that of *Romeo and Juliet* because of its invocation of death of Hero. Also, in this regard, *Much Ado About Nothing* also shares many features with Shakespeare's late plays or 'the romances' such as *Cymbeline* and *Pericles, Prince of Tyre,* and, most notably, *The Winter's Tale,* which critics also assign to be a genuine tragicomedy or romance. Like Hermione in *The Winter's Tale,* Hero too stages a false death only to come back to life once her beloved has repented the manner in which he treated her.

The adaptations of *Much Ado* and *The Taming of the Shrew* that are the subject of this analysis are both produced by BBC's *Shakespeare Retold* series and, unlike *Coriolanus* and *Macbeth,* they were produced by the same company with the intention of bringing Shakespeare closer to the contemporary audience. While Fiennes' film has managed to do the precisely same thing (perhaps most successfully of all the adaptations analyzed here) we must bear in mind that three out of four adaptations in this study are produced by BBC's *Shakespeare Retold* series with the intentional relocation of Shakespeare's plot and characters into the 21st century; this is why we have Macbeth the chef, Benedick and Beatrice the news anchors and Katherine the MP. The thread that runs through BBC's series advocates this relocation which, seen from the cultural materialist perspective, allows to examine and re-examine just how Shakespeare is relevant today. Fiennes' film was also relocated successfully into our modern world and it fits well as a commentary on the contemporary socio-political issues at hand, but the BBC's *Shakespeare Retold* series manages to bring a rather more subtle and intimate commentary that seems to underline a possible direction in which further Shakespearian adaptations might go – to feature the characters and the plot (or fragments thereof) supplied by Shakespeare and relocate the entire production into the context of modern time. Rather than having warlords, noblemen, noblewomen, knights and thanes we have a rather more subtle varieties of contemporary vocations such as chefs, journalists and politicians – all vocations that are perceived as prestigious in our time as were kings, queens, knights and thanes in Shakespeare's time.

While we cannot escape the impression that some plays by Shakespeare would perhaps not work if they were relocated in the manner BBC's adaptations are (it is indeed hard, not to say comic, to picture Coriolanus as a chef, journalist, or politician, for he was clearly proven not fit for the latter). The comedies *Much Ado About Nothing* and *The Taming of the Shrew* are well made to appeal to large audience that will, while enjoying Shakespeare's comedy at its best, undoubtedly recognize that the dark vision they entail is cloaked in light themes such as love and fidelity. However, the modern audience will also recognize that under the surface there is something troubling in these comedies and it is felt in both Percival's and Richard's adaptations.

Much Ado About Nothing is generally considered one of Shakespeare's best comedies, because it combines elements of great hilarity with more serious meditations on honor, shame, betrayal and courtship. Like other comedies including *The Taming of the Shrew, As You Like It* and *Twelfth Night, Much Ado About Nothing,* though overshadowed with darker concerns, is a rather joyful comedy that ends with multiple marriages and no deaths. Although one of the features of Shakespearean comedy is that no one dies, it would be a mistake to assume that death is absent from this kind of comedy. Often, Shakespeare's comedies are more accepting of death than his tragedies, treating death as part of the natural cycle of life. *Much Ado About Nothing* is no exception in this regard, when we see Hero pretending to die of humiliation we see that death is more vividly presented here than in any of Shakespeare's other comedies. The crisis that lies at the center of *Much Ado About Nothing* troubles many readers and viewers, since the play creates a very strong sense of anger, betrayal, hatred, grief, and despair among the main characters. Although the crisis ends quickly, *Much Ado About Nothing* sometimes seems only steps away from becoming a tragedy.

Although the young lovers Hero and Claudio (or Hero and Claude in Percival's adaptation) provide the main motivation for the plot, the courtship between the older, wiser lovers Benedick and Beatrice is what makes *Much Ado About Nothing* so memorable to may readers and theater goers. Benedick and Beatrice argue with delightful wit and whimsical remarks as Shakespeare develops their journey from pure antagonism at the beginning to sincere love and affection for each other at the end. Since Beatrice and Benedick have a history behind them that adds a great weight to their relationship by making them unique in all of Shakespeare, both Beatrice and Benedick are portrayed as older and more mature than the typical lovers we would meet in Shakespeare's comedies, though their unhealthy competitiveness at the beginning reveals them to be childish beginners when it comes to matters of love. The common history of Beatrice and Benedick is nicely added into Percival's adaptation:

> Beatrice in "Much Ado" is a case in point, a witty, intelligent woman who brings out the worst in her man by besting him in their war of words. Sarah Parish ("The Wedding Date") plays Beatrice, and Damian Lewis ("Band of Brothers," "The Forsyte Saga") plays Benedick, a vain, charming television personality who is hired to work alongside the woman he once dumped. There is a hint of sadness veining this version of Shakespeare's romp. The story begins with a flashback to Beatrice and Benedick three years earlier getting ready for a tryst: she scatters rose petals on her bed; he packs a bag and scuttles out of town. (Stanley 2006)

Furthermore, the verbal games that occur frequently in the BBC adaptation resemble the ones of Katherine and Petruchio from *The Taming of the Shrew*. Both Katherine 'the shrew' and her husband Petruchio exhibit wry humor and witty remarks that foreshadow the ones Shakespeare will use in *Much Ado About Nothing*.

> *The Taming of the Shrew* relies heavily on accepted dramatic conventions, and it approaches traditional farce in many respects. It lacks the depth of Shakespeare's later comedies, but it also foreshadows them; Katherina in particular anticipates Beatrice in *Much Ado About Nothing*. (Boyce 2005: 559)

The characteristics include lighthearted and slapstick humor, disguises, deception and a happy ending in which most of the characters come out satisfied. The lightheartedness of these romantic comedies contrasts sharply with the darker humor (evoking anger, betrayal, hatred, grief, and despair that are at the center of the play). Like *Much Ado About Nothing, The Taming of the Shrew* focuses on courtship and marriage, but, unlike *Much Ado*, it devotes a great deal of attention to married life after the wedding. The other comedies usually conclude with the wedding ceremony itself as is very much the case with *Much Ado*. The interesting thing about *The Taming of the Shrew* is that it deals with what happens in the married life of two young people. Here, one should take note that the marriages in the BBC's *Shakespeare Retold* adaptations is always shown between young couples at the beginning of their marriage (a good example of this kind of a situation in another adaptation is again *Macbeth* where we have a very young modern couple). In casting young British actors such as Shirley Henderson, Rufus Sewell, Jamie Murray (*The Taming of the Shrew*) as well as Sarah Parish, Damian Lewis, Billie Piper (*Much Ado About Nothing*) to play Shakespearian heroes, the BBC production targets the young audiences who will easier identify with their problems. However, *The Taming of the Shrew* is a rather 'difficult' comedy to be identified with since many critics have commented on its misogynic attributes – from the process of Petruchio's 'taming' of Katherine to 'the shrewdness' as such. Of particular worry to 16th century society were "shrews" or "scolds"—that is, gossipy wives, who resisted or undermined the assumed authority of the husband within a marriage. A large number of plays of the time address related topics: the taming of shrews by their husbands or the public punishment of scolds and other women who defied patriarchy. One could say that in challenging the patriarchic system that generates male dominance Katherine is one of the first examples of female resistance and originality ushered in by Geoffrey Chaucer's Wife of Bath of *The Canterbury Tales*:

> Here it may be worth pausing for a moment to reflect on the meanings of the word "shrew", which meant, in order of historical appearance,
>
> - a wicked, evil-disposed, or malignant man; a mischievous or vexatious person; a rascal, a villain;
> - the Devil;
> - a thing of evil nature or influence;
> - a person, especially (now only) a woman given to railing or scolding or other perverse or malignant behavior; frequently a scolding or turbulent wife.
>
> (Garber 2004: 66)

In some of this literature, it is difficult to distinguish between behavior that is being parodied and behavior that is presented as an ideal to which we can be loyal. This ambiguity may also be found in *The Taming of the Shrew*, which manages to circumvent the dominant chauvinistic behavior while simultaneously reaffirming its social validity in a given society. This play, very much like *Much Ado About Nothing*, celebrates the quick wit and fiery spirit of its heroes (primarily its heroines) and the manner in which this has been brought forth to the adaptations is quite interesting. The 'shrew' Katherine is a British MP and her shrew political verbosity that so much aids her in the Parliament and with her party is a major reason why she is not married

– men are rather terrified of her. Here she is depicted as a strong and independent woman that, although being difficult to the extent that it is parodied, is not fulfilled in the sense that's he is married. She is only 'truly fulfilled' if she takes a husband as her sister did. In *Much Ado About Nothing* we have a similar situation with the verbose Beatrice and Benedick who switch their roles of lord and lady; their verbosity finds a good place in a Wessex television studio (Kidnie 2009: 105) where this antagonistic couple makes great use of this situation by playing puns as they did in the play:

> "Much Ado About Nothing," (…) transfers Shakespeare's comedy from Messina to a television studio in Wessex; when Benedick overhears his colleagues discussing his chemistry with Beatrice, it is through a microphone left open on the set (Stanley 2006)

Their interaction in the studio seems to invoke other films, the romantic comedies with similar twists. The contemporary romantic notion of love is preserved in both adaptations as it had been in the adaptations before.

In the theoretical overview of the introduction chapter there was an extensive list of major Shakespearian adaptations wherein the earlier adaptations of *Much Ado* and *The Taming of the Shrew* alike were mentioned. *The Taming of the Shrew* adaptations have usually managed to flaunt the chauvinistic sentiments displayed in the play and this is also the reason why the theme of 'the shrew' managed to enter the world of film thus developing a romantic comedy or the screwball comedy; whether portraying 'the shrew' loyally to Shakespeare's original as Franco Zeffirelli did in his 1967 adaptation or relocating it so as to fit the younger audience – by making her as a stuck up high school girl like Gil Junger did in his 1999 *10 Things I Hate About You.* Brian Percival's adaptation is more similar to Junger's because it does attempt to make it fresh and accessible to the wider range of audience. The genre of the romantic comedy, most notably the screwball comedy, has elements within its structure that are present in both *Much Ado About Nothing* and *The Taming of the Shrew.* This type of comedy basically developed as a subgenre which distinguishes itself for being characterized by a female that dominates the relationship with the male central character, whose masculinity is challenged. One of the main traits of a screwball comedy is that its plot, just like the plot of plays like *Much Ado* and *The Taming of the Shrew*, features plot lines that involve courtship and marriage. Courtship and marriage are indeed the mutual ground for these two comedies and this issue also becomes a great similarity between the two when viewing the adaptations. The cultural materialist approach renders the plays as well as the adaptations through the issues of power and the manner in which power relations operate within these two plays; who has the power; who uses power; to whom is the power denied. Naturally, there is another aspect of cultural materialist analysis that cannot be escaped when eyeing the Percival's and Richard's adaptations – the cultural significance of the romance comedy. The romance comedy, slapstick and screwball comedy all emerged from plays like *Much Ado* and *The Taming of the Shrew* wherein we have romantic couples who share a fair amount of differences and, very frequently, a love-hate relationship that is ultimately resolved with a happy ending. The crucial concern with kind of comedy is that the differences that the couples exhibit are celebrated, even when they are made to appear as if they are ridiculed.

The crucial issues that will be illuminated within this analysis regarding *Much Ado About Nothing* and *The Taming of the Shrew* are manner power relations function in the plays and adaptations alike. The gender politics operates through language and Beatrice and Katherine, heroines of their respective plays, make great use of language by defying the patriarchic system that is at play. This has been incorporated into the adaptations as well by making a twist on the issues of gender; for instance, Petruchio in the BBC adaptation assumes the role of father who stays to raise children while Katherine pursues her career. Also, the manner in which the romantic comedy has developed from plays like *Much Ado* and *The Taming of the Shrew* will also be discussed by drawing a parallel between the genre of the screwball comedy and the ensuing twist on the genre of romantic comedy that came to life with the BBC *Shakespeare Retold* series.

Much Ado About Nothing and The Taming of the Shrew: Power Relations and Gender Hierarchy

Both *Much Ado About Nothing* as well as *The Taming of the Shrew* exhibit power relations between a wide spectrum of characters. Most notably, in the core of both of these comedies there is a power struggle that takes place between the male and the female characters. Language that the male and female characters use in their courtship is ridden with innuendos and deliberate ambiguities which, in turn, produce comic effect. However, beneath this comic surface, both *Much Ado* and *The Taming of the Shrew* address issues of power relations within the gender hierarchy. A very important aspect that ties all four plays in this analysis is the manner in which power operates within the hierarchy of gender politics. The power relations described in the previous chapter – between Macbeth and Lady Macbeth as well as between Coriolanus and his mother Volumnia lead us to construe the claim that in these two tragedies the male characters were dependent on the approval of the female characters for both Lady Macbeth and Volumnia are considered among the strongest female characters in all Shakespeare (with the inclusion of Rosalind from *As You Like It* and Cleopatra from *Anthony and Cleopatra*). The immense power of their words as well as the manner in which Lady Macbeth and Volumnia affect Macbeth and Coriolanus respectively has earned them an everlasting place in literature as women who defy patriarchy and who are quite capable of enacting power through the powerful men they dominate. This is important to mention because the female characters from the comedies *Much Ado About Nothing* and *The Taming of the Shrew,* Beatrice and Katherine respectively, dominate their plays not by enacting power through men as Lady Macbeth and Volumnia do very subtly, but by using language as a means of emancipation and self-empowerment. Beatrice does not wish to let Benedick into her life because of their troubling past; she does not want to be reminded of her pain and she finds in language she employs a variety of witty remarks that, although sounding fun and whimsical, have the intent to mask her feelings. Similarly, Katherine does not want to let Petruchio in her life because she does not need a man to command her and in her language she uses quips and insults that not only serve to deliver laugh but that also mask Katherine's feelings of self-doubt and jealously of her eligible sister Bianca who has no problems finding a husband:

> The scriptwriter Sally Wainwright reformed Shakespeare's play by relocating it into the domain of British political life; the shrew Katherine Minola (played by Shirley Henderson) is an MP, her sister Bianca (Jaime Murray) is "a pampered supermodel and perfume spokeswoman who swans across Europe with her manager-entourage trudging behind an overladen luggage trolley" (Pittman 2011: 158); while Petruchio, the 16th earl of Charlburry, and can be classified as another instantiation of the laughably eccentric titled classes (Pittman 2011: 162)

Language imposes itself as a means of challenging the system of patriarchy and the manner in which power is distributed therein:

Shakespeare's continuing interest in certain kinds of interpersonal relationships, like those between apparently compliant and apparently defiant women, the pleasures and dangers of the "language lesson", and the love banter of married or engaged couples, a war of words that will resound delightfully through plays from *Taming* to *much Ado About Nothing* to he teasing equality of Hotspur and Lady Percy in *Henry IV, Part 1*. (Garber 2004: 58)

Katherine seems not to be in a need of a husband, but the patriarchic system implies that she needs to marry. Beatrice on several occasions states that she cannot find a husband suitable for her (she needs someone to match her wit and only Benedick can do that), but her elderly uncle Leonato tells her "By my troth, niece, thou wilt never get thee a husband / if thou be so shrewd of thy tongue" (*Much Ado About Nothing* II, 1). It seems that the patriarchic system demands of the women to forfeit their language and to make it accommodative to men. Katherine and Beatrice challenge this system within their respective plays by extensive usage of the same kind of language that the patriarchic system prohibits – the one of spite. Katherine constantly insults and degrades the men around her, and she is prone to wild displays of anger, during which she may physically attack the men enrages her. Her anger sometimes makes her similar to Coriolanus for these two characters exhibit great rage indeed; also both of them are both antisocial and prone to outbursts of anger. Though most of the play's characters simply believe Katherine to be simply ill-tempered, it is certainly plausible to think that her unpleasant behavior stems from her unhappiness with her life. She may act like a shrew because she is miserable and desperate but beneath veneer of anguish lies a very sympathetic character. The scriptwriter of BBC's *The Taming of the Shrew* Sally Wainwright has made attempts to make Katherine Minola understandable in this regard and accessible to modern audience:

Katherine is presented as a physically and verbally abusive Member of the Parliament who is prone to making a public spectacle of herself. (…) In keeping with a range of critical and theatrical interpretations, this production variously implies as the source of her anger sibling rivalry, parental neglect personal eccentricity, a lack of sexual interest in men (her mother warily asks if she 'shops around the corner') and pent-up sexual frustration, with quite a lot made of the fact that she has never had an offer of marriage, has never been in a relationship of any account, and at thirty-eight is still a virgin. (…) By multiplying possible causes for her anti-social behavior, Wainwright makes Katherine's violent proclivities legible through the ready caricature of the career woman driven by a competitive edge that, in its single-minded ruthlessness, come to seem grotesque. (Kidnie 2009: 106)

There are many possible sources of Katherine's unhappiness that are as well displayed in the play as well: she expresses jealousy about her father's treatment of her sister Bianca, but her anxiety may also stem from feelings about her own undesirability in the eyes of men, the fear that she may never win a husband or her loathing of the way men see and treat her. Her sister Bianca (played by Jamie Murray) is the complete opposite:

> Bianca is the sensual, appealing and, unlike her sister Katherine, empowered woman who is in "command of her sexuality" (Kidnie 2009: 107) while her flame Lucentio, who tutors her in Italian, without the command of the English language, is "objectified as the subplot's sexually desirable, silent marriage partner" (ibid.)

In short, Katherine feels out of place in her society. It is perhaps apt therefore that Katherine is indeed relocated into an environment where her motivations may be better understood for that precisely was done with the BBC's *Taming of the Shrew*:

> Of all Shakespeare's comedies, *The Taming of the Shrew* most overtly reinforces the social hierarchies of its day. Lacking the gendered inversion of power and the poetic complexity of Shakespeare's romantic comedies, this early play might seem less likely to capture the imagination of modern audiences and producers, we might expect it, like its farcical companion *The Comedy of Errors*, to be filmed infrequently and almost obligatorily as part of canonical projects such as the BBC TV Shakespeare series. Quite the converse is true. More than eighteen screen versions of the play have been produced in Europe and North America, putting Shrew in a select league with "the big four" tragedies, and outpacing those comedies scholars usually dub more "mature. What accounts for this frequent

reproduction of an anachronistic plot premised on the sale of women (Henderson, quoted in Burt & Boose 2003: 120).

Due to her great intelligence and independence, Katherine, like Beatrice, is unwilling to play the role of the maiden daughter. She clearly abhors society's expectations that she should obey her father and men in generally. At the same time, however, Katherine must see that, given the cruelty of her social situation (the patriarch society she lives in), her only real hope for happiness in the world lies in finding a suitable husband. These inherently conflicting impulses may lead her to even greater misery and fits of ill temper. A vicious circle ensues from this unhappy circumstance: the angrier she becomes, the less likely it seems she will be able to able to perform her prescribed social role; in turn, the more alienated she becomes socially in defying the patriarchic system, the more her anger grows because she sees herself alone and unhappy. Beatrice, although not as angry as Katherine but similarly bitter because of her relationship to Benedick also exhibits traits of resistance towards the patriarchic system. She challenges the system by making herself unavailable to men – even my mocking their inadequacies. Unlike her foil in the play, Hero, she is outspoken, incompliant and uncompromised – the qualities that make her one of the most likeable and memorable characters in Shakespeare. Though she is close friends with Leonato's daughter Hero the two could not be less alike. Whereas Hero is polite, quiet, respectful, and gentle and is under the influence of the patriarchic system, Beatrice is feisty, cynical, witty, and sharp in her defense against the same system of patriarchy that has made Hero its

141

compliant servant. Beatrice keeps up a "merry war" of wits with Benedick, a lord from Padua in similar fashion as Katherine wages her "war of words" with lord Petruchio from Verona. The play suggests, as Percival's adaptation delightfully displays, that she was once in love with Benedick but that he disappointed her (even broke her heart) and their relationship has gone for the worse ever since that moment. Now when they meet, the two constantly compete in an exchange of clever insults.

Another common thing that Katherine and Beatrice share is that behind their mask of bitter and witty use of language directed at men, in their core both of them are delightfully tender and lovable characters. Although she appears hardened and sharp because of her experience with Benedick, Beatrice is really a vulnerable woman. Once she overhears Hero describing that Benedick is in love with her (Beatrice), she opens herself to the sensitivities and weaknesses of love, as does Benedick. Beatrice is a prime example of one of Shakespeare's strong female characters. She refuses to marry because she has not discovered the perfect, equal partner and because she is unwilling to lose her liberty and submit to the will of the patriarchic society. It is interesting how similar this makes her to Katherine. When Hero has been humiliated and accused of violating her chastity, Beatrice explodes with fury at Claudio for mistreating her cousin. In her frustration and rage about Hero's mistreatment, Beatrice rebels against the unequal status of women in Renaissance society. "O that I were a man for his sake! Or that I had any friend would be a man for my sake!" she passionately exclaims: "I cannot be a man with wishing, therefore I will die a woman with grieving" (IV.1). This instance was caught well in Percival's adaptation:

> (...) the television script sticks fairly closely to the play. In Act IV Beatrice is so enraged by Claudio's ill-treatment of her cousin Hero that she exclaims: "O God, that I were a man! I would eat his heart in the marketplace." In Wessex, Hero is the weather girl, and Beatrice hollers, "I swear if I were a man I would eat his heart." (Stanley 2006)

This undertone of earnest and profound sincerity is one of the reasons why *Much Ado,* like *The Taming of the Shrew*, is much more than a comedy. It gives us an insight into the complex characters far beyond the whimsical surface. The verbal folly, however, adds the comic weight to the plot and it masks the motivations of the characters by introducing comic relief. For example, in the famous scene where Petruchio and Katherine meet, Petruchio establishes that he is Katherine's intellectual and verbal equal in everything by making him an exciting change from the easily dominated men who normally surround her:

> PETRUCHIO: Come, come, you wasp, i'faith you are too angry.
> KATHERINE: If I be waspish, best beware my sting.
> PETRUCHIO: My remedy is then to pluck it out.
> KATHERINE: Ay, if the fool could find where it lies.
> PETRUCHIO: Who knows not where a wasp does wear his sting? In his tail.
> KATHERINE: In his tongue.
> PETRUCHIO: Whose tongue?

KATHERINE: Yours, if you talk of tales, and so farewell.

PETRUCHIO: What, with my tongue in your tail?

> (*The Taming of the Shrew* II.1)

This exchange between the two main characters occurs during their first meeting. Their conversation is an extraordinary display of verbal wit, with Petruchio making use of sexual puns in order to undermine Katherine's anger. Other characters frequently compare Katherine to a dangerous wild animal that needs to be tamed, and in this case, Petruchio calls her a wasp. She replies angrily that if she is a wasp, he had better beware her sting. He replies to this confidently that he will simply pluck her sting out thus rendering her unable to harm him. In saying this, Petruchio basically challenges to Katherine, foreshadowing his intent to tame her. Petruchio considers himself, as the other men consider him, to be a tamer who must train his wife, and most of the men secretly suspect at first that her wild nature will prove too much for him. Interestingly, Benedick from *Much Ado* equates marriage with the man being tamed:

> The savage bull may, but if ever the sensible Benedick
> bear it, pluck off the bull's horns and set them in my
> forehead, and let me be vilely painted, and in such great letters
> as they write "Here is good horse to hire" let them signify under
> my sign "Here you may see Benedick the married man.

> (*Much Ado About Nothing* I, 1)

Marrying would mean sacrificing his independence and Benedick finds the prospect of losing it either foolish. It is a strong enough intuition to make him feel queasy about marriage altogether. Unlike Petruchio,

Benedick does not wish to marry until he is made aware of the fact that he is in love in Beatrice. The same character was caught in Percival's adaptation but with a contemporary twist:

> Benedick prides himself on being an eternal bachelor, until cupid strikes. "Love is just one of those things a man grows into," he tells himself. "Like jazz. Or olives." (Stanley 2006)

Benedick is an entertainer (a great reason why the scriptwriter of BBC's *Much Ado* David Nichols made him into a news anchor) and because he is so invested in performing for the others, it is not easy for us to tell whether he has been in love with Beatrice all along or whether he falls in love with her suddenly during the play. Benedick's refusal to marry does appear to change over the course of the play, once he decides to fall in love with Beatrice. *Much Ado,* like *The Taming of the Shrew,* is imbued with metaphors regarding the process of taming. To tame is to establish power over someone and to exercise power in an obvious manner for everyone to see, for instance by shaming Hero by accusing her of adultery or shaming Katherine on her wedding day. Both of these acts occur publicly – for the loss of honor is worst that can happen. Shakespeare's time, a woman's honor was based upon her virginity and chaste behavior. This is where the double standards are clearly visible because for men honor depends on male friendship and, unlike a woman, a man could defend his honor by fighting in a battle or a duel. As a woman neither Hero nor Katherine can seize their honors back. Hero must comply with the slander that Claudio casts onto her while Katherine must go through the wedding ceremony with Petruchio who dressed like a clown only to spite her and to show her that, regardless of her feisty nature and superb wit, she must obey or she will ruin her only chance to wed and become accepted into society.

Much Ado shares its sentiments with The Taming of the Shrew because the play is also filled with metaphors involving the taming of wild animals. In the case of the courtship between Beatrice and Benedick, the symbol of a tamed savage animal represents the social taming that must occur for both 'untamed' souls (Beatrice and Benedick) to be ready to submit themselves to marriage. Beatrice's vow to submit to Benedick's love by "[t]aming my wild heart to thy loving hand" makes use of terms from falconry, suggesting that Benedick may become master of Beatrice's heart (III, 1). In the opening act, Claudio and Don Pedro tease Benedick about his aversion to marriage, comparing him to a wild animal. Don Pedro quotes a common saying, "In time the savage bull doth bear the yoke," meaning that in time even the savage Benedick will surrender to the taming of love and marriage (I.1). Benedick mocks this sentiment, professing that he will never submit to the will of a woman. At the very end, when Benedick and Beatrice agree to marry, Claudio pokes fun at Benedick's reluctance. He is suggesting that Benedick is afraid to get married because he remembers the allusion to tamed bulls:

> Tush, fear not, man, we'll tip thy horns with gold,
> And all Europa shall rejoice at thee
> As once Europa did at lusty Jove
> When he would play the noble beast in love.
> (Much Ado About Nothing V, 4)

Beatrice, likewise, abhors marriage:

> Beatrice bluntly disdains love, sneering, "I had rather hear my dog bark at a crow than a man swear he loves me" (1.1.120–122), but her first words (1.1.28–29) have already betrayed her interest in Benedick, although she covers it with a veneer of witty insults and teasing. She has suffered through an earlier unhappy romance with Benedick, as she suggests in 1.1.59 and 2.1.261–264, and her barbed wit is plainly defensive, disguising her true feelings even from herself. Her brashness is nicely contrasted with Hero's reticence in 2.1: Hero is twice prompted about her response to the expected courtship of Don Pedro, and on both occasions Beatrice's comments about marriage prevent her reply. Tricked into believing that Benedick loves her, Beatrice immediately discards her cynicism, saying, "contempt, farewell, and maiden pride, adieu!" (3.1.109–110) (Boyce 2005: 447-448)

The comic twist ensues when it turns out that these two loveable characters find that they are very much in love with each other. The role of matchmaker in this case is given to the elusive Don Pedro, who is the noblest character in the play's hierarchy. He resembles the Duke from *Measure for Measure* in the sense that he is like an agent that propels the plot; in fact he is the one that initiates the scenes where Benedick and Beatrice realize that they are in love with each other. Percival made a delightful twist in his adaptation by assigning the role of Don Pedro to the director at the news studio thus acknowledging his role as a 'director' of Beatrice's and Benedick's newly inflamed romance. It is his idea to convince Beatrice and Benedick that each is in love with the other. By doing so he is able to bring the two competitors together. He orchestrates the whole plot and he truly justifies why Percival has made him play the role of director because he is the 'director' this comedy of wit. Ultimately, because of Don Pedro's plan to put them together, Beatrice and Benedick are able to fall in love. Beatrice and Benedick both share their power only when the element of love in the play becomes clearly visible. This is what allows for the 'happy ending' at the end of the play. Petruchio, unlike Benedick, has to get married in order to secure his financial future:

> The marriage of Katherine and Petruchio enacts the economic and class aspirations of romance comedy in which one partner quite often climbs the class ladder through romantic union; in this case, the *Retold* episode attempts to equalize that rise since Katherine moves into the aristocracy through her husband and Petruchio gains financial salvation through his wife, a mutually beneficial exchange similarly traceable to Early English social customs. (Pittman 2011: 162)

His motivation for marrying Katherine is money. However, during the course of the play he actually falls for Katherine and proves a good husband. His behavior is extremely difficult to decipher but above all, Petruchio is a comic figure, an exaggerated persona who continually makes the audience laugh. And though we laugh with Petruchio as he 'tames' Kate, we also laugh at him, as we see him satirize the very gender inequalities that the plot of *The Taming of the Shrew* ultimately upholds. After the wedding, Petruchio and Katherine's relationship becomes increasingly defined by the rhetoric of domestication. Petruchio speaks of training her like a "falcon" (falconry imagery again) and plans to "kill a wife with kindness":

> What is at stake here is the taming process. No matter how stubborn Kate proves. Yet would I pull her down and make her come / As hungry hawks fly unto their lure. Petrucio then goes on describing how he will deny her sleep with device summed up as "Another way I have to make my haggard, / To make her come and know her keeper's call" (Dessen 2002: 204)

Petruchio specifies that the shrewish wife, like a falcon or a haggard, must be trained in order to look upon or "come unto" her lure; Petruchio moreover invokes that the power to tame Katherine is given to him by the patriarchic society which undermined the role of the woman. Petruchio was given the hand of Katherine in marriage by her father Baptista who, seemingly, controls the fate and happiness of his daughter:

> Thus in plain terms: your father hath consented
> That you shall be my wife, your dowry 'greed on,
> And will you, nill you, I will marry you.
> Now Kate, I am a husband for your turn,
> For by this light, whereby I see thy beauty—
> Thy beauty that doth make me like thee well—
> Thou must be married to no man but me,
> For I am he am born to tame you, Kate,

149

And bring you from a wild Kate to a Kate

Conformable as other household Kates.

Here comes your father. Never make denial.

I must and will have Katherine to my wife.

(*The Taming of the Shrew* II.1)

Since her father has agreed and the dowry has been settled, Katherine's consent is not needed, for Petruchio will marry her whether she likes it or not ("will you, nill you, I will marry you"). Petruchio even explicitly declares that "I am born to tame you, Kate," further employing the language of animal domestication by calling her a "wild Kate"—a pun on "wildcat"—that he will "tame." Although Katherine consents to marry him, she does not cease to challenge both the system that has allowed for this transaction to occur and her fate with new husband which her father had put into Petruchio's hands.

This passage embodies not only the fiery conflict between Petruchio and Katherine, but also the sexual attraction underlying it. It also extends the play's ruling motif of domestication, as Petruchio describes Katherine as a wild animal that he will tame. Perhaps this passage displays best the reason why the screwball comedy derives such great humor from ambiguous situations like the interplay between Petruchio and Katherine. The screwball theme embodied in wry and ambiguous humor just like in romantic comedies and this passage makes us forget about the interplay of power in this play by seemingly making the two characters equal.

However, the process of 'taming' that occurs in *The Taming of the Shrew* is rather described as 'torment' of Katherine by Petruchio.

Petruchio's forcible domestication of Katherine is in every way designed to show her that she has no real choice but to adapt to her newly acquired social role as a wife. The motif of domestication is broadcasted in the play's title by the word "taming." A great part of the action consists of Petruchio's attempts to cure Katherine of her antisocial hostility. Katherine is thus frequently referred to as a wild animal that must be domesticated. It must be difficult for Katherine to adapt to Petruchio's zany ideas but for her it is important to become a wife in the system of patriarchy but playing the role at least means she can command respect and consideration from others rather than suffer the rejection she receives as a shrew. Having a social role, even if it is not ideal, must be less painful than continually rejecting any social role at all. Thus, Katherine's eventual compliance with Petruchio's self-serving "training" appears more rational than it might have seemed at first: by the end of the play, she has gained a position and even an authoritative voice that she previously had been denied. The domestication also takes place in *Much Ado About Nothing* (the symbols of tamed savage animal was mentioned above as well as Beatrice's vow to Benedick) but this domestication of Beatrice never takes place:

> There is something in Beatrice's temperament that must always evade domestication. Her fury that she cannot be a man in order to avenge Claudio's slander upon Hero goes well beyond gender politics in authentic savagery:

> > I am not approved in a height of a villain, that hath slandered, scorned, dishonored my kinswoman? O that I

were a man! What, bear in her hand until they come to take hands, and then with public accusation, uncovered slander, unmitigated rancour – O God that I were an man! I would eat his heart in the market-place. (IV, 1)

(Bloom 1998: 199-200)

Even though Beatrice does not allow for domestications, her foil in the play, Hero, does. Even though Hero is ultimately vindicated, her public shaming at the wedding ceremony is too terrible to be ignored. The public shaming of Hero is similar with the wedding shaming of Katherine. The ridiculous outfit Petruchio wears to his wedding with Kate symbolizes his control over her. Simply by wearing the costume, he is able to humiliate her. It may be shameful for Kate to be matched to someone in such attire, but she knows she has no choice if she does not wish to become an old maid. She consents to let the ceremony proceed, even with Petruchio dressed like a clown, and thus she yields to his authority before the wedding even begins. These kinds of humiliation are perpetrated by the dominant male characters (Claudio and Petruchio) who wield considerable power. The powerless women have to take the punishment (Katherine must marry Petruchio) while Hero is called a "rotten orange" (IV.1), and to her father Leonato she is a rotting carcass that cannot be preserved: "the wide sea / Hath . . . / . . . salt too little which may season give / To her foul tainted flesh!" (IV.1). Shame is also what Don John hopes will cause Claudio to lose his place as Don Pedro's favorite the fear of public shame (or be exact, the pressure of the hierarchic system). Shame is a form of social punishment closely connected to loss of honor. A product of an illegitimate sexual coupling himself, Don John has grown up constantly reminded of his own social shame, and he will do anything to right the balance. Percival's adaptation features the character Don who is a miserable alcoholic with the sole intention of having Hero for himself (Don and Hero had a brief affair, as we can gather from the BBC' adaptation).

Both *Much Ado* and *The Taming of the Shrew* feature two different couples within each of the play. The key difference between them is that one couple is conventional and strictly adheres to the social code while the other couple is completely the opposite – unconventional and defiant towards everything and anything. Claudio and Hero from *Much Ado* are clearly the couple that is rather conventional, young and inexperienced while Beatrice and Benedick are the mature yet childishly whimsical couple that steals the show from Claude and Hero, who are supposed to be the center of *Much Ado*. Similarly, the subplot of *The Taming of the Shrew* entails the love story of Katherine's sister Bianca and Lucentio. This couple, when compared to the hectic and turbulent Katherine and Petruchio, is clearly fades into the background. The reason behind the lesser popularity of the couples Claudio / Hero and Bianca / Lucentio is because these couples are consenting to the patriarchic system that imbues them. The only exception is Lucentio's resistance to his father to marry Bianca after all. The dominant couples in both comedies are the ones that similarly attempt to defy or expose the manner in which power relations functions and these are the ones that have the strong female characters.

When analyzing the two plays / adaptations from the cultural materialist perspective, we must take into account the titles of both plays for both titles are suggestive of the plot that ensues in both plays and adaptations. Unlike the previous two plays /adaptations *Coriolanus* and *Macbeth* where the title clearly specifies the tragic protagonist of each play, here we have a different situation where the titles are much subtler and foreshadowing of the plot that will ensue. *Much Ado About Nothing* signifies in its very title that 'nothing' is the play's prime signifier. Much ado is indeed done because of an act that did not occur; much fuss is done about nothing. Hero's alleged unfaithfulness propels the plot of *Much Ado* and it almost transforms it into a tragedy. The 'happy ending' in the final act that literally plucks the play from the fangs of tragedy could not be welcomed more by the audience that realizes that indeed all the fuss in the play was for *nothing*. However, there is a different meaning of the word *nothing*; In Shakespeare's time, the "nothing" of the title would have been pronounced "noting." Thus, the play's title could read: "Much Ado About Noting":

> The title phrase has had a celebrity virtually independent of the play itself, but itse relevance to the dramatic action and language is far more direct than the phrase might at first suggest. A fuss about a trifle. "Big deal" might be more our modern counterpart. (Garber 2004: 379)

This is quite interesting because many of the players participate in the actions of observing, listening, and writing, or noting. In order for a plot depends on instances of deceit to work, the characters must note one another constantly. When the women manipulate Beatrice into believing that Benedick is in love with her, they hide themselves in the orchard so that Beatrice can better *note* their conversation. They do so precisely because they know that Beatrice loves to eavesdrop, they are sure that their plot will succeed: "look where Beatrice like a lapwing runs / Close by the ground to hear our conference," notes Hero (III.1.) However, as Marjorie Garber notes, there was wide spectrum of the meaning of the word "nothing" and it extended far beyond "noting":

> But "nothing" in the English Renaissance had a wide range of meanings, all of them specific or pertinent. "Nothing" meant a thing or person not worth mentioning – as Don John will say, with hidden intent, that Hero's misdeeds are "not to be named... not to be spoke of" (4.1.94), which is literally true since in fact they do not exist. "Nothing" could also mean someone of little worth like the foolish Watch headed by Dogberry. "Nothing" paradoxically, also could mean "everything" or "all", since its sign was the full or empty circle, and in this play whose most characteristic mode of language is paradox, much ado is indeed made about everything. (Garber 2004: 379)

Indeed, much ado, as Garber claims, is done about everything in this play and much ado is also done in Percival's adaptation and all because of a scheme of the villainous Don (John) the main plot of the slander of Hero is propelled. As Garber sharply observes, the paradoxical aspect of *Much Ado* is something that is well caught by the language that is employed. The paradoxical element of the play is also that the subplot (love between Beatrice and Benedick) becomes much more interesting than the main plot (love between Hero and Claudio). However, this play is considered one of Shakespeare's best precisely because of the element of comedy which is mixed with tragedy (note that the love between Claudio and Hero verges on tragedy while Beatrice's and Benedick's wooing occurs exclusively under their merry banter of their "merry war of words"). *Much Ado,* because of the main plot (which is paradoxically second to the subplot) contains elements that threaten to make it a tragedy. There is a very good example of this both in the play as well as in the adaptation when, after slandering of Hero, Beatrice tells Benedick to "kill Claudio":

> This is a play that several times comes dangerously close to tragedy. Beatrice's command to her lover, "Kill Claudio", is a turning point in more ways than one, as actors and directors must struggle to retain the sincerity of the moment of their previous banter. (Garber 2004: 390)

The title of *Much Ado About Nothing,* as we see, has considerably more meaning to it, as does the play itself. This is another example why the modern productions of this play have so many times given rebirth to this play over and over again – because it finds its audience very easily in our contemporary world. *The Taming of the Shrew,* likewise interesting in its title at least as much as *Much Ado,* has the above mentioned process of 'taming' in its core. Whether the taming occurs literally through the harsh hand of Petruchio or whether 'the taming' is actually a synonym for the taming of Katherine's wild heart is an issue that has been debated as long as the play was is existence. From the love quarrels of Petruchio and Katherine we might deduce an entire spectrum of contemporary marriages that bear resemblance to this couple. The modern productions of this play have generally remained faithful to Shakespeare's original although in the BBC's

Shakespeare Retold we have Richard's adaptation wherein the shrewish Kate Minola (Shirley Henderson) marries Petruchio (Rufus Sewell) and at the end we have a rather delightful twist wherein Kate, as modern 21st century working woman unlike the 16th century obedient wife, goes on to pursue her career in politics while Petruchio, with a smile on his face stays at home taking care of their children. Shakespeare has in this manner transcended the barriers of gender politics as well as the patriarch hierarchy. Richard's adaptation addresses this aspect precisely from the point of view of the 21st century.

The issue of power relations set in both *Much Ado About Nothing* and *The Taming of the Shrew* explores the economic aspects of relationship and marriage. *Much Ado* the play, as well as the adaptation features the relationships between characters that are of similar or equal social stature. Lord Benedick and Lady Beatrice as well as Lord Claudio and Lady Hero belonging to the same social classes are, despite Don John's scheming, quite easily made into happy matches – two lords and two ladies. One might think of Lord and Lady Macbeth as the example of the same social class here. In the adaptation, Percival's Benedick and Beatrice are news anchors, employees in the same profession, both of same social stature and both single in their thirties. Claude (Claudio) and Hero are likewise employees of the Wessex media house and they also belong to the same social class. Even is the malevolent Don (John) works in the studio as their equal. On the other hand, the power relations in *The Taming of the Shrew* are not as visible and simple as they are in *Much Ado*:

The fact that roles representing various social ranks are all performed by stage players (all "low" by early modern standards of status) and that women's roles on the public stage in England were performed by boy actors underscores the degree to which social order and hierarchy are both cultural fictions and material realities of life. It is the inevitable and fruitful tension between these two aspects, the fiction and the fact that animates the plot, the comedy, and the cleverness of this play. (Garber 2004: 58)

Kate Minola from the adaptation is a powerful woman in the British parliament while Petruchio, although lord of Charlbury, is of a poor financial situation and he *must* marry in order to maintain his financial situation. This is similar to Shakespeare's original but the twist here is that Kate is given much more power (political power) than is the case in the play. This modern twist allows us to examine and re-examine how the modern power struggles occurs. *The Taming of the Shrew* emphasizes the economic aspects of marriage—specifically, how economic considerations determine who marries whom: a influential politician can marry a lord with an influential title. The adaptation tends to explore romantic relationships from a social perspective, addressing the institutions of courtship and marriage rather than the inner passions of lovers; Petrucio *must* marry and Kate *must* marry; Petruchio *must* come to financial security while Kate *must* marry a title. Moreover, the adaptation focuses on how Petruchio's and Kate's courtship affects not just the lovers themselves, but also their and their friends. In the play, while the husband and the wife conduct the marriage relationship after the wedding, the courtship relationship is negotiated between the future husband and the father of the future wife. As such, marriage in the play, just like in the adaptation, becomes a transaction involving the transfer of money. In the play, Lucentio wins Bianca's heart, but he is given permission to marry her only after he is able to convince Baptista that he is fabulously rich. Had Hortensio, the other suitor of Bianca, offered more money, he would have married Bianca, regardless of whether she loved Lucentio or not. Richards' adaptation, unlike Shakespeare's original, features not just the process of 'taming' but it provides the context fro the cultural materialist examination of male insecurity:

> Male insecurity provides the context and motivation for Katherine's final speech of wifely duty. Asked for her opinion during the family row occasioned by her sister's demand for a pre-nuptial agreement, and noticing her husband flinch when her mother insists that 'We live in an age of divorce', Katherine announces to Bianca that she should be grateful to have a husband to take care of her. Her depiction of a marriage in which the husband works to support a wife who stays as home watching television notably bears little relation to the show's narrative circumstances or conceptual framework, given that Harry is the only man in the room (apart from Lucentio's translator) who works for a living. Both Lucentio and Petruchio are supported financially by their high-flying wives, with Petruchi, as becomes clearer in the programme's 'after-story', staying at home to raise their children while Katherine goes on to become Prime Minister. (Kidnie 2009: 109)

The cultural materialist rendering of *The Taming of the Shrew* invokes a new, modern reading that manages to appear as if removed from the original in its misogynic sentiment but the moderns twist by its scriptwriter David Nichols manages to make the adaptation an comedic experience that transcends the 16th century and brings a refreshing breeze of its slapstick comedy well into the 21st century along with the refreshing form of gender politics that, although offering the plot the political background, manages to provide the comic relief for its lovable couple – Kate and Petruchio.

Much Ado About Nothing along with their most prominent couple, Beatrice and Benedick, although featuring great comic relief through the "merry war of words" between the lovable couple, has underlying darker shades which makes it a different experience than *The Taming of the Shrew*. *Much Ado,* similarly to *Coriolanus* and *Macbeth,* features its plot against a raging war. However, unlike *Coriolanus* where war is something that happens in the foreground, in *Much Ado* and *Macbeth* war is in the background. In the previous chapter, we saw that the scene introducing the blood stained Macbeth is structured against a war that the Scottish thanes are fighting. Indeed, war is the key theme in *Coriolanus, Macbeth* and *Much Ado About Nothing* alike for war as a political conflict serves as a vehicle of establishing power relations. We commented on the manner of how such power relations operate in *Coriolanus* and *Macbeth* but the manner in which war operates in *Much Ado* is different since this play deals with the aftermath of war:

> War is a key theme here, war and its aftermath. The opening scene in Messina presents a society of women and older men (Leonato, his daughters Hero and his niece Beatrice) from which

the young men have departed to fight – a world, that is, waiting
for return of youth and love (Garber 2004: 376)

Although one could make the case that war in *Macbeth* is shown as
over by the time Macbeth usurps the throne. However, in *Macbeth* we
have a state of constant and perpetual war that ensues upon
Macbeth's usurpation of the throne so clearly one might suggest that
Macbeth, like *Coriolanus,* is drenched in blood and violence of war.
Much Ado About Nothing, being a comedy, must tackle the thematic of
war differently than tragedies like *Macbeth* or *Coriolanus,* even
differently than histories like *Richard II, Henry VI Part 1,2 and 3, Henry
VIII* or even *King John* but, as Garber suggests, war is here in its
aftermath. In the opening scene we have a world bereft of youth for all
the young men had departed to war. The happy return of the men to
Messina foreshadows rather happy and joyous occasion that features
masquerade and falling in love. War serves here as the mere
background, like a landscape in the background on a painting. The
1993 movie *Much Ado About Nothing* directed by Kenneth Branagh
subtly uses the background of Sicily just in the same manner: the
landscape features the background for the plot. When Don Pedro of
Aragon (played by Denzel Washington), signor Claudio (Robert Sean
Leonard) and signor Benedick (Kenneth Branagh) ride into the
beautiful scenery of Messina they signify the end of war and the
beginning of other conquering: Claudio's conquering of Hero (Kate
Beckinsale). This is again the action conquering that brings *Much Ado*
into correlation with *The Taming of the Shrew.* Furthermore, throughout
Much Ado, images of war frequently symbolize verbal arguments and
confrontations. At the beginning of the play, Leonato relates to the

161

other characters that there is a "merry war" between Beatrice and Benedick: "They never meet but there's a skirmish of wit between them" (I.1.). When Benedick arrives and banters with Beatrice (played by the superb Emma Thompson), their witty exchange resembles the blows and parries of a well-executed fencing match. Similarly to what happens in *Coriolanus* and *Macbeth* in the terms of body politics, both *Much Ado* and *The Taming of the Shrew* alike feature the conquering of women; it is as if conquering of the female body is equated with the conquering of a country. Petruchio has to 'tame' Katherine in order to secure his finances – which are mainly the reason why wars are fought. Similarly Claudio's slander of Hero evokes the image that her body is already something that belongs to him (Leonato had given him the hand of Hero in marriage as did Baptista give Katherine's hand to Petruchio) – the body of the woman is where the battle takes place. The female body needs to be domesticated (*The Taming of the Shrew*) so as to fit the social hierarchy and it needs to be pure and unstained (*Much Ado About Nothing*) or else it loses its appeal. The body politics operates subtly in both plays, cleverly undermining the influence of body politics while at the same time making the body, the female body to be exact, a ground where the battle for ultimate signification will ensue. The four happily married matches from the two plays (Katherine and Petruchio, Bianca and Lucentio, Beatrice and Benedick and Hero and Claudio) are matched because the female bodies have ultimately been conquered; a happy ending and the promise of love have indeed tames the wild hearts of the female characters. However, the defying Beatrice and Katherine from their respective play continue to prove as agents of resistance. In her final speech on marital obedience, Katherine says:

162

My mind hath been as big as one of yours,

My heart as great, my reason haply more,

To bandy word for word and frown for frown;

But now I see our lances are but straws,

Our strength as weak, our weakness past compare,

That seeming to be most which we indeed least are.

Then vail your stomachs, for it is no boot,

And place your hands below your husband's foot,

In token of which duty, if he please,

My hand is ready, may it do him ease.

(The Taming of the Shrew V.2)

Katherine says that women's bodies are soft and weak because their inner selves should match them and that women should thus yield to their men. She then tells Bianca and the widow that, in her time, she has been as proud and as headstrong as they are ("My mind hath been as big as one of yours, / My heart as great"), but now she understands that "our lances are but straws," implying that their weapons prove insignificant and improperly used. However, when Katherine says a few lines before this: "I am asham'd that women are so simple" (V.2.) wherein she subtly renders the following advice to women regarding their husbands to be ironic. One would have to be very literal-minded not to hear an underlying tone of irony and sarcasm in this line and it is precisely this instance that requires a very good actress to deliver this kind of advice (Elizabeth Taylor in Zeffirelli's 1967 *The Taming of the Shrew* comes to mind here), for Katherine is advising women on how to rule absolutely while at the same time feigning obedience and servitude:

True obedience here considerably less sincere than it purports to be, even if sexual politics are to be invoked, (...) as Kate teaches not ostensible subservience but the art of her own will, a will considerably more refined than it was at the play's start. This speech's meaning explodes into Petruchio's delighted (and overdetermined response);

Why, there's a wench! Come on, and kiss me, Kate!

(Bloom 1998: 35)

Like Katherine so too does Beatrice manage to evade domestication and the great reason why she manages to do so is because she has managed to find a partner that is equal to her. And although none of them can escape the powerful law of marriage in our social system ("No", Benedick says in act 2, "The world must be peopled"), ultimately both find happiness in an equal marriage. Both Beatrice and Benedick are so wise that their love will grow into a mature marriage. They are so beautifully lively and independent that even when they speak sweetly to each other, they never lose their bantering spirit as is seen in the closing scene of *Much Ado:*

BENEDICK

A miracle! Here's our own hands against our hearts. Come, I will have thee; but, by this light, I take thee for pity.

BEATRICE

> I would not deny you; but, by this good day, I yield
> upon great persuasion; and partly to save your life,
> for I was told you were in a consumption.

> (*Much Ado About Nothing* V, 4)

Beatrice, like Katherine, is a very strong woman in the sense that she is extraordinarily independent and courageous. She seems confident that she does not want to submit to marriage in order to obtain her self-efficiency. It is clear that she is very much aware of the exiting social pressure and the expectations of her getting married. At one point in the play, Leonato says to her: "Well niece, I hope to see you one day fitted with a husband" to which she delightfully replies: "Not until God make men of some other metal than earth" (II, 1) She simply refuses to submit to the social pressure and she manages to remain resistant towards it as does Katherine with her ironic speech at the end of her play. Their way of thinking resembles the was most modern women nowadays contemplate marriage and relationships and Percival's and Richard's adaptations have managed to capture both of these fantastic characters that emerge from their respective plays as bigger than life and in doing so they enabled both Kate Minola and Beatrice to become truly the modern women of our century that Shakespeare envisioned in the 16th. If Lady Macbeth and Volumnia were envisioned as archetypes of 'wife' and mother' respectively in their respective plays, then Beatrice and Katherine are likewise archetypes of female independence and resistance to societal pressure to consent to patriarchic customs of marriage. Even though one might argue that Macbeth and his Lady have one of the most stable marriages in Shakespeare, a similar case can made for *Much Ado About Nothing* where the marriage between Beatrice and Benedick, unlike the marriage of the Macbeths, upholds the promise of a 'happy ending' as does the marriage between Katherine and Petruchio. In this regard, featuring the likeable characters, comic relief and an appealing setting, both *Much Ado* and *The Taming of the Shrew* have ushered in the trend that has come to be identified with the genre of the romantic comedy.

Much Ado About Nothing and The Taming of the Shrew: Models of a Modern Romantic Comedy

As was mentioned in the introduction in this section, both *Much Ado About Nothing* and *The Taming of the Shrew* are considered prime examples of the genre of romantic comedy: the lighthearted slapstick humor, deception and, ultimately, the happy ending that ensues at the end of both comedies, all of this combined makes them a significant part of this genre. At the end of both *Much Ado* and *The Taming of the Shrew* most characters come out satisfied. Both plays offer elements of the screwball comedy which developed as a subgenre which distinguishes itself for being characterized by a female that dominates the relationship with the male central character, whose masculinity is challenged. Both Katherine in *The Taming of the Shrew* as well as Beatrice in *Much Ado* are, as was argued above, strong females that challenge the masculinity of males. One of the main traits of a screwball comedy is that its plot, just like the plot of plays like *Much Ado* and *The Taming of the Shrew*, features plot lines that involve courtship and marriage.

Courtship and marriage are indeed at the core of both *Much Ado* and *The Taming of the Shrew*. The romantic comedy has developed from plays like this and, over the course of the years the banters of Katherine and Petruchio as well as Beatrice and Benedick has indeed become prototypical of the ensuing dialogues that are to be found in movies from *The Philadelphia Story* (1940) to *Love Actually* (2003) thus developing a romantic comedy or the screwball comedy. *The Taming of the Shrew* has made a long was from one adaptation to another, whether portraying 'the shrew' loyally to Shakespeare's original as Franco Zeffirelli did in his 1967 adaptation or relocating it so as to fit the younger audience – by making her a stuck up high school student conceived as "a heinous bitch" by her peers as Gil Junger did in his 1999 *10 Things I Hate About You*. Brian Percival's adaptation is more similar to Junger's because it does attempt to make the play fresh and accessible to the wider range of audience. The genre of the romantic comedy, most notably the screwball comedy, has elements within its structure that are present in both *Much Ado About Nothing* and *The Taming of the Shrew*. This type of comedy basically developed as a subgenre which distinguishes itself for being characterized by a female that challenges the masculinity of the male central character, which results in series of comic situations.

The battle of the sexes, something that is invoked in the modern romantic genre we know today, had been already incorporated by

Shakespeare several centuries ago first with *The Taming of the Shrew* and later in *Much Ado About Nothing*. Both of these plays feature self-confident and rather stubborn female protagonists and the plot that is centered around the theme of marriage. Another common element is the quick exchange of witty remarks and as we can gather from the banters of Katherine and Petruchio as well as Beatrice and Benedick, this aspect is more than featured in both *The Taming of the Shrew* and *Much Ado About Nothing* for the series of witty remarks literally never cease in both plays. These elements that feature the romantic screwball theme in both plays have been the main reason behind so many adaptations of both of these plays. The aforementioned adaptations of *The Taming of the Shrew* by Zeffirelli (1967) and Junger (1999) could not be more different but somehow they both manage to address the issue of love and romance while preserving the original plot and characters that Shakespeare envisioned centuries ago. The adaptation of *Much Ado About Nothing* (1993) by Kenneth Branagh also managed to capture the feisty nature of its most prominent couple Beatrice and Benedick (which Emma Thompson and Kenneth Branagh played convincingly) wherein the romantic plot was clearly featured in the battle of the sexes

When Kenneth Branagh adapted Shakespeare's comedy *Much Ado About Nothing* for the screen in 1993, he had the good sense to shape it like a romantic comedy. Romantic comedy may be a modern genre, but *Much Ado* has all the same elements – most importantly, two lovers who begin as antagonists and find their way through the friction to a romance that is deepened by the challenges they pose to one another. It also has some of the funniest romantic banter in the history of theater and Emma Thompson, as the unstoppably witty Beatrice, blazes through those lines with the exuberant physicality of an English screwball heroine. (Shubert 2012)

Benedick and Beatrice are always at the center of our attention both in Branagh's adaptation as they are in Percival's. They get the most stage time, as well as the majority of the best lines because they are the romantic centerpiece of the play. With their constant bickering each of them hopes to expose the frailties of the other and this universal theme of the battle of the sexes has been around ever since, Furthermore, not only do Beatrice and Benedick attempt to expose the frailties of each other, but they also try to expose the frailties of his or her entire gender. These interchanges are early examples of what would become the fast-paced exchanges in modern screwball comedy. Although some of the couple's verbal swordplay in Percival's adaptation is rendered more loosely this does not mean that it has lost its edge but only that it had become more adapted to our contemporary world. As the camera light turns green, Beatrice says sweetly, to Benedick "You really do put the W into anchorman, don't you?" (Stanley 2011),

With *Much Ado About Nothing*, Shakespeare also creates, along with Katherine and Petruchio, the first example of the romantic convention wherein the two romantic leads that love to hate each other. Beatrice thinks that there is no man who is worthy of her; there is no perfect match for her, she says:

What should I do with him—dress him in my apparel and make him my waiting gentlewoman? He that hath a beard is more than a youth, and he that hath no beard is less than a man; and he that is more than a youth is not for me, and he that is less than a man, I am not for him.

(*Much Ado About Nothing* II.1.)

Those who possess no facial hair are not manly enough to satisfy her desires, whereas those who do possess beards are not youthful enough for her. Comic notions, one might say conundrums, like this will usher in the prototypical strong female character that, seemingly self-sufficient, turns out to be a sympathetic character in need to love. Benedick likewise abhors marriage, but when he is tricked into believing that Beatrice loves him, he swiftly changes his mind on the entire prospect of marriage:

They say the lady is fair. 'Tis a truth, I can bear them witness. And virtuous—'tis so, I cannot reprove it. And wise, but for loving me. By my troth, it is no addition to her wit—nor no great argument of her folly, for I will be horribly in love with her.
(*Much Ado About Nothing* II.3.)

Benedick ponders this news and concludes that the best thing for him to do now, at the point where he knows that Beatrice loves him, is to return this love: "for I will be horribly in love with her" (II.3). This line produces a comic relief as it seems preposterous that someone would fall "horribly" in love with another person after simply mentioning that person's virtues. The choice of the word "horribly" fits so perfectly in this play because it *horribly* accentuates the comic aspect of Benedick's decision. Not only does he decide to return Beatrice's love,

170

but he does so to the point of outmatching her with his love. The choice of "horribly" could also echo the merry war Beatrice and Benedick have been fighting with their wits because "horribly" evokes the imagery of war. There always existed an element of competition between the two that was embodied in the imagery of "merry war" of words. It is not enough for Benedick to simply answer to Beatrice's passions; he must, in the fashion of the romantic comedy, outdo them, perhaps in order win the competition and, in doing so, win Beatrice's heart and "the merry war of words" altogether.

That Beatrice and Benedick are "tricked" into loving each other is only possible because that love already resides in their hearts – they are both sympathetic characters that make us like them from the first moment. This romantic notion of the main protagonists is the reason why we, as viewers want for them to be together – we *want* a 'happy ending' because we want to see both of them happy at the end. Beatrice and Benedick use their mutual animosity to cover their true feelings of love. Of course, *Much Ado About Nothing*, like *The Taming of the Shrew,* is never simply just a romantic comedy. Rather, the play creates a lighter, more frivolous counterpart to some of his darker tragedies. For example, as it was mentions earlier in this chapter, *Much Ado* is compared to plays like *Romeo and Juliet* we see a lover pretend to be dead (as Hero pretended to be dead), in this fashion hoping for a romantic reconciliation with the man to whom she is supposed to marry. Unlike that tragedy, however, the lover (Claudio) realizes his mistake at the end and, a happy ending is possible only because of this lucky resolution at the last moment.

The Taming of the Shrew addresses the romantic comedy genre in a similar manner as does *Much Ado*. Richards' version, although exhibiting the notion of power relations and featuring a rather submissive Kate as did the original, adheres more closely to the prescribed formula of the romantic comedy:

> When interviewed on the DVD, Director David Richards remarks of *Taming*: "The original play is very big, quite bawdy in some places, comedy. It isn't a piece of naturalism, and we took that same note for our adaptation of it." Series producer (Diedrick) Santer adds: "In the original play, it's a really hard story. You know (Petruchio) really just beats her (Katherine) into submission. In our version, we make it bit more equal. It's sort of the taming of two shrews, and by the end they're slightly more balanced and happy people. In Santer's description of the *Retold* approach, *Taming* adheres closely to the formula typical of the romance comedy film in which two difficult, even anti-social, characters soften and alter through the alchemical experience of love. " (Pittman 2011: 157.158)

Here we have a more contemporary, fragmented approach to *The Taming of the Shrew* which entails showing both Kate and Petruchio as "shrews" which need to embark on a voyage of self-discovery in order to have a happy marriage. The modern approach that Richards attempted in his adaptation has been generally well received as the adaptation instantly found its audience and received critical acclaim because it features common links between the original play and the modern adaptation written by Sally Wainwright:

In *Taming* (...) the distance one occasionally registers between the modern script and Shakespeare's language is usually a function of the Petruchio character's eccentric, larger than life personality – 'I've come to wive it wealthily in Padua', he declares inexplicably to 'Harry' (Hortensio) as he slumps into a chair in the middle of a comfortable living room in what looks like Bettersea, London. Such practices of modernization are by now unfamiliar strategies of production, with the works interpreted – some might say 'adapted' (...) – in order to make them feel contemporary (Kidnie 2009: 105-106)

Although Petruchio uses a number of techniques in order to 'tame' Kate. As previously mentioned, he proves to her that he can match her verbal acuity and quick wit, and then he uses his extreme confidence. "Kiss me, Kate" is a phrase that is used frequently in the play and, as we saw in the introduction the 1953 musical adaptation directed by George Sidney makes use of this phrase as does Richards in his adaptation:

PETRUCHIO: Kiss me, Kate.

KATHERINE: Up yours, weirdo!

Because Petruchio attempts to tame Kate in the rhetoric of love and affection, it is impossible for her to confront him with outright anger, and the possibility remains that the two will develop a genuinely loving relationship in the future. Of course, *The Taming of the Shrew* is a comedy, and Petruchio's techniques are somewhat fantastical. But both Kate's apparent willingness to comply with Petruchio's demands and Petruchio's desire to court Kate's love make considerably more logical sense if we accept the explanation that, beneath their conflicts, they legitimately love one another. Katherine and Petruchio banter on every step of the way, similarly like Beatrice and Benedick, while Petruchio's insistence that she be 'tamed' has offers considerable relief, especially when Katherine complies to do his bidding. "I'll tame the bitch!" says Rufus Sewell's character over the phone to his friend Harry (Hortensio). The 'shrew' seems to be 'tamed' in the famous passage in the play where Petruchio orders her to say that the sun is really the moon. Tired, hungry, and weary of their conflicts, Katherine at last succumbs to Petruchio as she declares that he might as well define reality for her from this point forward:

> Then God be blessed, it is the blessed sun,
> But sun it is not when you say it is not,
> And the moon changes even as your mind.
> What you will have it named, even that it is,
> And so it shall be still for Katherine.
>
> (*The Taming of the Shrew* IV.6.)

With this, Petruchio's victory over Katherine becomes inevitable: after this, she can no longer resist his authority, and her taming is nearly complete. Similarly to this scene, we have the wedding scene, where Petruchio also exercises his power over Katherine by embarrassing her whit his clownish attire; there is the comic effect here in which of the groom, ridiculously dressed, is humiliating his bride. However, there is an underlying reading of the play here which signifies that the clownish attire Petruchio wears is a symbol of the transient nature of clothing. In the play, Petruchio declares that Katherine is marrying *him* and not his clothes. This romantic notion indicates that the man beneath this clothing is not the same as the foolish clothing itself hence making Petruchio a romantic hero. Richards' adaptation features a rather similar scene, with Petruchio's appearance made more identifiable with the contemporary audience. The comic relief ensues with the decision of making Petruchio wear a blend of contemporary fashion accessories, mainly extravagant:

> The comedy derived from such a decision emerges as the parties arrive for the service. A long shot of the church exterior shows a white Rolls Royce carrying Katherine and her sister approaching from left as a moped ridden by Petruchio and his friend Harry pulls up from the right. Slightly worse for drink, Petruchio sports eyeliner, nail polish, high heeled kinky boots, fishnet tights, riffled shirt, a kilt, and a long black velvet coat. Quick cuts and handheld shots create the expected instability that mimics Petruchio's drunken staggering as he lurches off the moped. (Pittman 2011: 161)

This scene puts us, the viewers of the 21st century, directly within the adaptation itself for the fashion accessories that Petruchio sports are familiar to us (they even manage to evoke, briefly, the image of the 1967 Zeffirelli adaptation wherein Richard Burton wears his attire of rags in a similar fashion much to the dismay of Elizabeth Taylor's character). The audience is included to revel in this blend of fashion accessories that Petruchio has on. The fragmented pieces like this are what allows for the adaptation to evoke the original play over and over again. This usage of the modern approaches is also quite visible in Percival's adaptation of *Much Ado About Nothing* wherein we have the plot centered around a televisions studio and the audience can clearly see what is going on behind the cameras. This modern approach to inviting the audience to partake in the plot by familiarization of certain modern trends of contemporary phenomena (as television) only amplifies the strength of the plot that evokes romance through the fragmented style of filming:

> This artful and fragmented filming style raises as an unanswered question the identity of the third presence in the park, implying solely through camerawork the presence of supernatural forces. *Much Ado*, however, is perhaps the film which integrates this self-conscious visual play most fully into its methods of story-telling: *Much Ado* is not only on television, but *about* television and its production in, and for, and increasingly mediatized culture. The programme's self-reflexive attitude is captured in the many scenes set in an imagined Wessex television studio. The action of the drama takes the viewer behind the camera, as it were, to watch the roles played by producer, director, editors, make-up artists, and newscasters in the production and broadcast of local regions. Cameras and teleprompters, frequently featured in the television frame, become ordinary parts of the programme's mise-en-scene, technical jargon used in the production gallery while the show is live on air cues opening credits, commercial breaks, and movement between cameras, and one watches the constant interaction between gallery and studio floor that happens by means of headset, earphone, and two-way intercom.

Occasion human error intrudes to disrupt the show's smooth broadcast: Don, the newscast's first director, is late on his cues, there is momentary confusion about which camera the meteorological reporter, Hero, is supposed to address, and the live broadcast suddenly cuts to an embarrassed Benedick caught checking for good in his teeth. (Kidnie 2009: 122)

Shakespeare's characters never seemed so close to us as they are in these adaptations because we manage to see ourselves in them. The familiar settings allow for this kind of identification that, in the case of *Much Ado About Nothing,* stretches to the usage of the very medium that is used to represent them.

The BBC's production of *Much Ado* likewise struggles with Shakespeare's comic marriages. In *Much Ado,* for example, Hero and Claude (Claudio) are never reconciled after his humiliation of her at the altar, the film playing with viewer expectations of the work of challenge the politics of romantic desire. The action shifts from the abandoned wedding reception to a hospital ward when Hero hits her head and falls into a coma. What follows that night when her friends and family leave the hospital is a version of the display of penance performed by the mourning groom outside of the tomb, there played as a bedside monologue between Claude and the unconscious Hero that is as familiar a trope of television hospital drama as is the nurse who finally enters to usher him firmly into the hall. As the camera tracks Claude leaving the ward, the soundtrack takes an ominous turn, lights start flashing at the nurses' station, and hospital staff rush past him towards the room he has just left; forcing his way back into the room, Claude discovers – at the same time as the viewer – Hero sitting up in bed, the filmic clues at first interpreted as evidence of death on fact marking her unexpected journey (Kidnie 2009: 109-110)

The medium of television is hence used not just as a means of adapting Shakespeare but also as a means of taking Shakespeare and making his characters and plot part of the television trope which, in turn, brings Shakespeare closer to the contemporary audience. The convention of the modern romance that is evoked in *Much Ado About Nothing* echoes in the ears of its modern audience by invoking one of the most famous pairs in romance combined with the new contemporary setting. Shakespeare indeed never looked and sounded more contemporary than when viewed as unrolling his plot in news studio. The image of Ralph Fiennes' Coriolanus taking a briefing from a soldier via Skype or his live interview in the TV studio come to mind here as being particularly revealing of the usage of technology that propels Shakespeare's plot and contemporizes its characters within the context of the 21st century.

The romantic comedy is indeed anticipated within Shakespeare's *Much Ado About Nothing* and *The Taming of the Shrew*. The contemporary adaptations by the BBC's *Shakespeare Retold* series follow the formula of the romantic comedy by employing all the aspects that are relevant for such a production. *Much Ado* features it happy ending as does *The Taming of the Shrew*:

> The ending of *The Taming of the Shrew* borrows something from the conventions of the romantic comedy film; in its closing montage of black and white photos, *Taming* makes use of the photographic epilogue, a staple of the happily-ever-after ethos of romantic comedy. (Pittman 2011: 164)

By employing realistic situations combined with utter unrealism Shakespeare's comedies, although featuring elements of deceit, jealousy, resentment and betrayal, the adaptations also offer comic relief which surpasses its darker shades. The 'taming' of Katherine by Petruchio is as unrealistic as are the scenes in the orchard where Beatrice and Benedick are made aware of their love for each other. However the love that these couples feel for each other is very much real and it provides a happy ending thus making it a romantic comedy we all know and love. It is the constant interplay of these kinds of realistic and utterly unrealistic expectations that we witness when we see a comedy in its purest. This is what Shakespeare did with his two plays featuring relationships and marriage and this thematic was adapted by Percival and Richards alike in their films. By employing the notion of this interplay between the characters and their contemporary surroundings, both comedies have attained the notion of the romantic since both feature a "happy ending" with a romantic twist as well as the principal plot and characters envisioned by Shakespeare as being apt for a comedy. Alenka Zupančić caught this notion as a symbiosis between realistic and unrealistic:

> (...) comedy involves a strange coincidence of realism (it is supposed to be more realistic and down-to-earth than, say, tragedy) and utter unrealism (defying all human and natural laws, and getting away with things that one would never get away with in "real life"). This unrealistic, "incredible" side of comedy is also related to its proverbial vitalism: a kind of undead, indestructible life, a persistence of something that keeps returning to its place no matter what... I would suggest that it is precisely here, in this utterly unreasonable insistence, that we find the true realism of comedy (Zupančić 2008: 217)

The realism in the adaptations of *Much Ado About Nothing* and *The Taming of the Shrew* is ever present and it is confronted by unrealistic twists that make it comical and worth wile. *Much Ado* and *The Taming of the Shrew* alike feature these characteristics and more than that for they both have unforgettable characters that make them stand out from many romantic comedies. The characters of Beatrice and Katherine are insomuch archetypical as are the characters of Lady Macbeth and Volumnia for all four feature strong female emancipated characters that managed to become larger than their plays. This indeed makes them as contemporary in our world as it does the characters of Macbeth and Coriolanus.

Although different in genres, all four adaptations feature characters that are incredibly modern in their attitudes as well as in their motivations which makes clear the reason as to why these plays were so easily accepted by the contemporary audience. It is indeed easier to identify with Beatrice and Katherine as being strong and emancipated women of the 21st century as it easier to perceive Macbeth and Coriolanus as men whose tragic flaw comes from their unsatisfied ambitions. Their problems and worries are as close to us as ours because in them we find pieces of our own desires and fears. The modernity of Shakespeare is hence made appealing to the modern audience precisely by incorporating the original themes used by Shakespeare and combining them with a fragmented approach wherein the characters and the plot remains essentially the same.

The appeal of Shakespeare has managed to remain strong amongst our contemporary culture as it was centuries ago because of the universal themes that still continue to be modern regardless of their age or their audience – whether in tragedies like *Macbeth* and *Coriolanus* or in romantic comedies like *Much Ado About Nothing* and *The Taming of the Shrew*. In both tragedy and comedy, as will be commented in the concluding remarks, Shakespeare excels in portraying the human – from raw human emotions in *Macbeth* and *Coriolanus* to delightful displays of wit and humor in *Much Ado* and *The Taming of the Shrew*. In Shakespeare's plays we find the ambitions, desires, fears, hopes and dreams that are, amongst many others, the bastion of emotions that constitute the human essence in its purest – to paraphrase Harold Bloom, he invented the human. That is the reason why we are so at ease to identify with his characters – because they speak to us about us, regardless of their time or culture because Shakespeare transcends time and the modern adaptations of his plays are the perfect example of his timelessness.

EPILOGUE

"He was not of an age, but for all time." This often quoted part of a poem was a verdict of Shakespeare's contemporary fellow playwright Ben Johnson on the Bard's timeless craft of writing. Being both "of an age" as well as "for all time", Shakespeare is the defining figure of the English Renaissance and a synonym for English literature:

> But if we create our own Shakespeare, it is at least as true that the Shakespeare we created is a Shakespeare that has, to a certain extent, crated us. The world is which we live and think and philosophize is, to use Ralph Waldo Emerson's word, "Shakespearized" (Garber 2004: 3)

The world we inhabit is "Shakespearized" to such an extent that he has become an integral part of our culture; he is quoted by politicians and celebrities alike. His ability to adapt his plot and characters so as to fit any time has proven universal.

This instance is what makes a cultural materialist reading of Shakespeare an incredible experience. In his plays he crafted incredible characters that perpetually question what it means to be human. This is the greatest reason as to why Shakespeare's plays continue to be performed nowadays and not just in the past; why he is loved and revered globally and not just in English-speaking countries;

why it is so easy to identify with his characters regardless of nationality or cultural differences. Shakspeare's adaptations have proven to be an excellent vehicle that transports the Bard's plays well into the 21st century. The characters of Coriolanus, Macbeth, Beatrice, Katherine as well as others from his original plays are well received in their modern adaptations. The question that was asked in the introduction, where the adaptations will go on from this point, finds it answer in the mixture if straightforward and fragmented interpretations that were conducted by directors like Fiennes, Brozel, Percival and Richards. *Coriolanus, Macbeth, Much Ado About Nothing* and *The Taming of the Shrew* are the most recent adaptations that meet this trend and there are several adaptations that are in development which will follow the blend of straightforward and fragmented concepts of these adaptations. The question of where the adaptations will go on will be briefly discussed as a means of opening up a new area of Shakespeare on screen research for other analyses that will surely follow. Another thing that is worth mentioning while remarking on these kinds of adaptations is their educational value; for Shakespeare is also represented in the classroom via his adaptations because they prove to be a fine resource of learning about his plays. Teachers worldwide use certain adaptations that make Shakespeare closer and more comprehendible to students. The cultural materialist practice hence puts Shakespeare in the center of our cultural and educational values. He transcends cultural barriers and brings out the universal traits of the human soul that are in common to all of us:

Shakespeare's influence, overwhelming in literature, has been even larger on life, and thus has become incalculable, and seems recently only to be growing. It surpasses the effect of Homer and Plato, and challenges the scriptures of West and East alike in the modification of human character and personality. Scholars who wish to confine Shakespeare to his context – historical, social, political, economic, rational, and theatrical – may illuminate particular aspects of the plays, but are unable to explain Shakespeare's influence on us, which is unique, and which cannot be reduced to Shakespeare's own situation, in his time and place. (Bloom 1998: 717)

His characters fall in love, and out of love, they like or dislike each other, betray each other, argue, fight and kill each other, they are angry, sad, happy, jealous, loyal, envious, heroic, distrustful, humble, untrustworthy, forgiving, deceptive – in a word: human; to an extent that is as uncanny as is the feeling we get when we see a tiny reflection of ourselves in one of his numerous portraits of the human soul. Indeed, his characters experience practically every human emotion you can think of, and every human situation which makes identifying with them inevitable. "I have a smack of Hamlet myself, if I may say so" wrote Samuel Taylor Coleridge. Goethe thought so too; and so did Sigmund Freud. (Garber 2004: 4).

Professor Harold Bloom, a great aficionado of Shakespeare and a self-proclaimed "Bardolator", in his book *The Western Cannon*, wherein he explore the relations between Shakespeare and the Cannon, Chaucer and Shakespeare, Milton and Shakespeare, Freud and Shakespeare, Joyce and Shakespeare, and Beckett, Joyce, Proust and Shakespeare, and which is really a celebration of Shakespeare as an individual as much as it is a celebration of literature in general, notes that we are all in Shakespeare because he is the corner stone of contemporary culture. Marjorie Garber agrees with this sentiment:

> Every age creates its own Shakespeare. Another way of saying this is to observe that Shakespeare serves a wide variety of cultural purposes, from political nationalism around the globe to modern-day instructions in "leadership" for business and corporate culture. (Garber 2004: 28)

This overwhelming influence of Shakespeare is deeply felt in contemporary culture through the medium of film and, as we could note in the first chapter, this influence is still felt in the latest adaptation (Fiennes' *Coriolanus*) as it was in the first adaptation (Tree's *King John*). Regardless of the time span between Fiennes' *Coriolanus* (2011) as being the latest and Tree's *King John* (1899) as being the first adaptation the audiences worldwide seem not to have had enough of Shakespeare. More than a hundred years (a hundred and twelve years, to be more exact) is the amount of time between these two films and this more than a century long period of time was filled with interpretations that ranged from faithful representations of the Bard's works to more fragmented and experimental films that drew on Shakespeare's works. During this period of time Shakespeare was on television and on film simultaneously; he was there from the very beginning of television. One can claim that Shakespeare on screen began from the same point as did the screening itself. In this regard, he is one of the few writers in the history of the world for whom it can be said that he was there from the beginning of the TV phenomenon *and* whose works still draw our attention even more so than they did today.

Our contemporary culture has embraced Shakespeare as well as his characters and plots – we *know* Shakespeare through the eyes of Hamlet, Othello, Macbeth, Coriolanus, Falstaff, Shylock, Caliban, Rosalind, Romeo, Juliet and others and the visual experience we get when we see them on the screen intensifies the feeling of familiarization with them and with their fates. Their charachters speak to us directly; regardless of the time they live in, they manage to speak to our circumstances; they allow us to relate to them. Shakespeare could not have anticipated that his plays would offer characters and plot that could be identifiable to such an extent. One could say that in portraying his characters, Shakespeare transcends the categories of time and place:

> What is often described as timelessness of Shakespeare, the transcendent qualities for which his plays have been praised around the world and across the centuries, is perhaps better understood as an uncanny timelessness, a capacity to speak directly to circumstances the playwright could not have anticipated or foreseen. Like a portrait whose eyes seem to follow you around the room, engaging your glance from every single angle, the plays and their characters seem always to be "modern", always be "us" (Garber 2004: 3)

187

This modernity that Garber notes is a spark of the universal spirit that Shakespeare gave unto his characters. In doing so, he gave them something that every generation of theatre goers *and* cinema goers alike can relate to. Our time is no exception from this rule. Indeed, our time is perhaps the best indicator of how Shakespeare has managed to gain such great attention. For even his plays that were not popular before have, as it seems, found their resonance in our modern times. A prototypical example of this is his tragedy *Coriolanus* which was, if we exclude T. S. Eliot's preferentiality for it as discussed in Chapter 3, never a very popular play. The contemporary audience has found the character of the crude and unrefined character of Coriolanus a trait that makes him 'modern' and this is indeed a character that is far removed from the likes of characters that have become synonymous with Shakespeare's main corpus and which are revered by critics and audiences worldwide; characters like Mark Anthony, Troilus, and Hamlet, who is Coriolanus' opposite in almost every aspect. Not to say that *Hamlet* is losing his appeal (diehard aficionados of the Danish Prince like Professor Harold Bloom would not hear of it) but perhaps time is coming for other tragic characters which bear a burden that is more identifiable to the man of the 21st century. The time we are living in is hectic and displays charachters that are men of action, men with the ability to act – Coriolanus and Macbeth are these men. Amidst the wars, famine, poverty, civil unrest and the threatening state of ever constant war characters other than the passive Danish Prince emerge; characters that are as cruel and gritty as the very world we inhabit. Coriolanus and Macbeth are precisely these types of emerging modernity. In their stories we unfortunately find similarities with our time and ourselves.

When we get a fragmented version of the same play wherein the plot and he characters are cloaked in the context of our contemporary world, then instantly these adaptations become something larger than merely plays written by a playwright that lived some five hundred years ago. Because of their universal appeal they become a critique of our everyday life. We identify with the problems of the characters and they become something that we can relate to. This is how Shakespeare manages to be relevant in our times:

Shakespeare is in a way always two playwrights, not one: the playwright of *his* time, the late sixteenth and early seventeenth centuries in England and the playwright of *our* time, whatever that time is. The playwright of *now*. (Garber 2004: 28)

His presence within our popular culture is something that has grown so familiar to us and this goes to such an extent that, it would be impossible to imagine our culture as it is without his influence.

The adaptations of *Coriolanus* (2011) and *Macbeth* (2005) are a testimony of Shakespeare's timelessness; both directors have managed to capture the essence of Shakespeare on screen and to transpose the compelling visual imagery from the page to the screen. Kenneth S. Rothwell summarizes this well as an effort of transferring Shakespeare to the cinema:

The history of Shakespeare in the movies has, after all, been the search for the best available means to replace the verbal with the visual imagination, an inevitable development deplored by some but interpreted by others as not so much a limitation on, as an extension of, Shakespeare's genius into uncharted seas (Rothwell 2004: 5)

As we could see in Chapter 2 this was no easy task to accomplish and Ralph Fiennes and Mark Brozel have undergone different methods to interpret their respective adaptations. Fiennes' adaptation relocates *Coriolanus* into the contemporary setting wherein we witness the decrepit modern Rome, ruled and ruined by corrupt politics and poor leadership. This image evokes our modern society and in doing so Fiennes gives a compelling critique to the modern political scene. Fiennes manages to question what we seek from our leaders today by rendering a centuries' old play that basically asks the same question. By even retaining the archaic expressions in the play, Fiennes masterfully structures the adaptation so as to sound alarmingly modern in our contemporary time. Brozel's *Macbeth* is, like other BBC's adaptations that were the subject of this analysis, both relocated (as was *Coriolanus*) and fragmented into a blend of familiar set pieces supplied by Shakespeare combined with a familiarizing contemporary setting that we can relate to.

The relocation that takes place in BBC's *Shakespeare Retold* series is taken a step further and that is felt in Brozel's *Macbeth* as much as in Percival's *Much Ado About Nothing* and Richards' *The*

Taming of the Shrew. Mark Brozel in his adaptation features a relocated chef Joe Macbeth who, along with his fiendish wife Elle, casts an uneasy shadow of ambition and appetite for power on the film as much as the original Macbeth and his Lady did centuries ago. In this modern relocation we are made aware of the dark ambition that runs in all of us and its destructive power. When rendered through the prism of cultural materialism, both *Coriolanus* and *Macbeth* reveal frameworks in which power relations operate in contemporary society; how the patterns of authority are play out in both adaptations (female empowerment through Lady Macbeth and Volumnia, the discourse on body politics); the manner in which Shakespeare is incorporated into popular culture.

The emphasis on female characters in all four adaptations reveals that the gender politics plays a significant role nowadays as it did several centuries ago. Figures like Lady Macbeth and Volumnia which, have become synonymous with female empowerment, resonate with modern audiences and their characters are revered as more contemporary than they were ever before. Beatrice from *Much Ado About Nothing* and Katherine from *The Taming of the Shrew* join this group of empowered and modern women perhaps even more so because Shakespeare wrote their plays before *Macbeth* and *Coriolanus*. In doing so Shakespeare could not have foreseen that he would create archetypes of modernity as much as he did with the characters of Coriolanus and Macbeth. It is no secret that Shakespeare's female characters have always taken husbands that were inferior to them. Some of examples of this are Helena and

Bertram from *All's Well That Ends Well*, Viola and Orsino from *Twelfth Night,* Portia and Bassanio from *The Merchant of Venice*, Rosalind and Orlando from *As You Like It* – all of these couples having female characters that are nobler, wittier and more sympathetic than their male counterparts. This is where *Much Ado About Nothing* and *The Taming of the Shrew* differ for these two plays, as we have seen in Chapter 3, offer rather similar male and female counterparts that fulfill each other delightfully in nobility and wit. Beatrice and Benedick from *Much Ado* and Katherine and Petruchio from *The Taming of the Shrew* are the modern types of romantic couples with their witty arguments, delightful wordplay and identifiable problems. This is what speaks to the contemporary audiences and they are responsive to this thematic. The evidence of this is the great reception of both Percival's *Much Ado* (2005) as well as Richards' *The Taming of the Shrew* (2005) in newspaper articles and other media. Shakespeare remains relevant and gives his critique of modern relationships and marriages.

Furthermore, in his tragedy *Macbeth,* Shakespeare likewise supplies perhaps his most famous set piece of equal partners in marriage that bear remarkable similarity with contemporary marriages. Brozel's adaptations, just like Percival's and Richard's, offers a set of young lovers, a couple young people who are married (or about t get married) and this image of youths getting married is rather significant for Shakespeare has been made revitalized – young actors are cast to play his characters and all this in the service of bringing him closer to the modern audience. BBC's *Shakespeare Retold* addresses the young audience and the series manages to evoke the interplay between the young and the old precisely by a fragmented plot and characters (played by young actors) that collide with the original thematic supplied by Shakespeare.

The enormous box office success of Shakespeare films, both relatively straightforward interpretations as well as fragmented adaptations, suggest that watching Shakespeare is at least popular as reading him. We have witnessed this in the Chapter 1 with the development of Shakespeare on screen from the very beginning in 1899 to the latest Fiennes' film in 2011. An important question that was asked in the introduction to this analysis is where the adaptations will go from this point on. Since we have covered the greatest milestones in Shakespeare on screen and focused heavily on all four adaptations that are the subject of this analysis, we have come to see that there is the fragmented aspect of Shakespeare on screen that is different than the straightforward adaptations and we could see segments of this fragmenting approach in all four adaptations, most notably in the BBC's *Shakespeare Retold* series wherein we have a complete relocation of both character and plot (unlike Fiennes' film wherein only the characters are relocated). This fragmented state of modernistic instances that collide with original Shakespeare allows for his charachters to move in our contemporary world and to act in a fashion that we can relate to. They *speak* to us in many ways because there are fragments of our culture and society that are incorporated within the very fiber of their adaptations. With such an approach directors like Fiennes, Brozel, Percival and Richards have opened up the way for other filmmakers to direct Shakespearian adaptations in a similar fashion.

The answer to the question of where the adaptations will go in the future could be seen in several adaptations of Shakespeare that are expected to be released in the near future[9]. The upcoming *Romeo and Juliet* (2013) adaptation will be a rather classic and straightforward story of "the star crossed lovers" with a supporting role of Paul Giamatti. However, there is also a fragmented take on *Romeo and Juliet* that is also scheduled to be filmed soon. It is titled *Rosaline* and it deals with Romeo's love interest before he meets Juliet. *Rosaline* will deal with the unseen girl of *Romeo and Juliet* and it will be relocated into a high-school setting (perhaps similarly like Gil Junger's *10 Things I Hate About You*). Percival's *Much Ado About Nothing* (2005) will surely be compared to the adaptation of the same play that is scheduled for 2013. Joss Whedon, the writer/director of the box-office hit *The Avengers* (2012) will be adapting a modern-day take on *Much Ado About Nothing. The Guardian* called it "the first great contemporary Shakespeare since Baz Luhrmann's *Romeo + Juliet.*[10]"

Macbeth will also be adapted into a thriller titled *Enemy of Man* wherein which tells of a war hero and his return home which offers him

---

[9] The adaptations that are listed below and their descriptions are available from: <http://www.shortlist.com/entertainment/films/all-you-need-to-know-about-forthcoming-shakespeare-movies> , see article titled *All You Need to Know About Forthcoming Shakespeare Movies*, accessed 15. Jan 2013.

[10] See <http://www.shortlist.com/entertainment/films/all-you-need-to-know-about-forthcoming-shakespeare-movies>

the lure of ambition thus beginning his gradual downfall. However, not just the cinematic adaptations will be featured; also a fragmented TV version of *Hamlet* is expected to be released. It will be titled *America's Son* and will be loosely based on *Hamlet*. It will focus on a Kennedy-style political family, featuring the death of the presidential candidate whose son investigates the 'accident'. As we can see, the trend for further Shakespearian adaptations will not cease to inhabit the silver screen any time soon. Quite the contrary, the adaptations of Shakespeare will continue to display the political, social and cultural critique of our contemporary world. One of the most intriguing adaptations expected is also not a far cry from the political arena – the Italian drama *Caesar Must Die* features an intriguing idea of several convicts who rehearse for a prison performance of *Julius Caesar*. The *Hollywood Reporter* is calling it "a fascinating encounter between theater and reality.[11]" Michael Radford and Al Pacino have had a fine collaboration on *The Merchant of Venice* (2004) and they have announced to film an adaptation of *King Lear* a few years ago. This project has been in development for a while and it seems that will see the light of day in 2013. Directed by Radford and starring Al Pacino as the tragic King Lear, this adaptation will very likely be a straightforward interpretation of one of Shakespeare's most famous tragedies.

After this brief overview of what adaptations will await us in this year and the following, we may see that the trend of fragmented and relocated Shakespeare will gain popularity. This is easily seen with Brozel's, Percival's and Richard's adaptation under the BBC's

---

[11] ibid.

Shakespeare Retold umbrella. Of course, the traditional straightforward interpretations are bound to be filmed in a continuation of the trend began by Laurence Olivier and upheld by Kenneth Branagh. The straightforward story that Fiennes delivers in *Coriolanus* (2011) is evidence enough that, although filming an adaptation that is faithful to Shakespeare's original and even retaining the original language, it is possible to undertake relocation into a contemporary setting.

Many of these adaptations, apart from being popular in the eyes of modern audience, are also used by teachers around the world when teaching Shakespeare. Teachers use the Shakespearian adaptations to talk about his plays because of the performative quality of the adaptations. There is the impossibility of assisting to theatrical performance of all the plays and this is where the adaptations become not merely a culturally significant phenomenon but an educative way of teaching Shakespeare and the way he is relevant nowadays. An appropriate example of this is Gil Junger's *10 Things I Hate About You* (1999) which is attempted to resonate so deeply with the young audience that it is actually set in a high school. However, there is a wide variety of quality straightforward adaptations that follow the plot. This also a reason why these adaptations are worth being studied and analyzed; not merely for their enjoyable qualities, even though most of them are not masterpieces of film, but because of the wide array of themes they speak of. Old and new audiences continually find certain traits that make these adaptations worth watching. Adaptations like *Coriolanus, Macbeth, Much Ado About Nothing* and *The Taming of the Shrew* are a consistent proof of this claim.

All four adaptations that are the subject of this analysis feature Shakespeare's complex characters set into the modern context of contemporary world. Because of their contemporariness they indeed speak to us about our own culture, politics and society. It is as if they were not conceived some five hundred years ago but made as fresh contemporary characters that depict the state of our society. Shakespeare's genius made his characters universally applicable to any situation and they find considerable resonance in our modern day and time. All four directors have managed to contextualize their respective plays into completely acceptable 21st century settings. In the fashion of cultural materialism the characters that inhabit these adaptations indeed become our contemporaries for they are at the foreground of contemporary issues and the adaptations keep them there – in the focus of today and the problems of politics and power. All this is contextualized with the politics of the body and the manner in which bodies are integral in the organic community that is that our contemporary society has become.

There are indeed so many details of today that are incorporated into the modern version of Fiennes', Borzel's, Percival's and Richard's adaptations. With the modernization of their plays, they become an immensely stronger medium that is able to hold the meaning that was forged several centuries ago in a brand new package and still not lose any of its sharpness. In the midst of world conflicts raging around the globe nowadays such a parable may be what we need – modern-day characters for our contemporary world.

BIBLIOGRAPHY:

1. Barry, Peter. "Beginning Theory" *An Introduction to Literary and Cultural Theory.* Aberyswyth, Wales: University Press 2002. eBook.

2. Bate, Jonathan. "Jonathan Bate: Skillful Remixes of the Bard for All Seasons". 9.12.2005.

3. Bate, onathan. *The Genius of Shakespeare.* London, Basingston, Oxoford: Picador (Pan Macmillan Ltd.), 1997. eBook.

4. Bloom, Harold. *Shakespeare: The Invention of the Human.* 1st ed. New York: Riverhead Books, Published by the Penguin Group (USA) Inc., 1998. Print.

5. Bloom, Harold. *The Western Canon: The Books and Schools of Ages.* 1st ed. New York: Riverhead Books, Published by the Berkley Publishing Group, 1994. Print.

6. Boose, Lynda, E., and Richard Burt. "Totally Clueless: Shakespeare Goes Hollywood in the 1990." Trans. Array *Shakespeare, the Movie: Popularizing the Plays on Film,*

Tv, and Video,. Lynda E. Boose and Richard Burt. 1st ed. New York: Routledge, 1997. Web. 9 Nov. 2012.

7. Borot, Luc. "Ideology as delusion: Bodies and politics in *Coriolanus*". IRCL- Montpellier 2007. Web. available

8. Boyce, Charles. *Critical Companion to William Shakespeare: A Literary Reference to His Life and Works*. Revised Edition. vol. 1&2. New York: Facts on File Inc.; Roundtable Press, 2005. eBook.

9. Branagh, Kenneth, dir. *Henry V.* Perf. Kenneth Branagh, Brian Blessed and Derek Jacobi. 1989. DVD. British Broadcasting Corporation (BBC); The Samuel Goldwyn Company;

10. Branagh, Kenneth, dir. *Much Ado About Nothing.* Perf. Kenneth Branagh, Emma Thompson, Keanu Reeves, Kate Beckinsale and Denzel Washington. 1993. DVD. American Playhouse Theatrical Films; The Samuel Goldwyn Company;

11. Branagh, Kenneth, dir. *Hamlet.* Perf. Kenneth Branagh, Julie Christie, Billy Crystal, Robin Williams, Judi Dench and Richard Attenborough.1996. DVD. Castle Rock Entertainment; Columbia Pictures;

12.Branagh, Kenneth, dir. *Love's Labor Lost*. Perf. Kenneth Branagh, Alessandro Nivola, Alicia Silverstone, Carmen Ejogo and Adrian Lester. 2000. DVD. Pathe Pictures International; Intermedia;

13.Brozel, Mark, dir. *Shakespeare Retold: Macbeth* . Perf. James McAvoy, Keeley Hawes and Joseph Millson. 2005. DVD. British Broadcasting Corporation (BBC); Horsebridge Productions Limited.

14.Bruster, Douglas. *Shakespeare and the Question of Culture: Early Modern Literature and the Cultural Turn*. New York, Houndmills, Basingstoke, Hampshire: Palgrave Macmillan, 2003. eBook.

15.Bulman, James C. *Shakespeare, Theory and Performance*. New York: Routledge 1996. Print.

16.Burnett, Mark Thornton, and Ramona Wray. *Screening Shakespeare in the Twenty-First Century*. Edinburgh: Edinburgh University Press, 2006. Print.

17.Burt, Richard, and Lynda E Boose. *Shakespeare, the Movie II: Popularizing the Plays on Film, Tv, Video, and Dvd*. 1st ed. New York, London: Routledge, 2003. Print.

18. Cartelli, Thomas, and Catherine Rowe. *The New Shakespeare on Screen*. 1st ed. Cambridge, Malden: Polity Press, 2007. Web.

19. Cartmell, Deborah. *Interpreting Shakespeare on Screen*. Houndmills, Basingstoke, Hampshire and London: Macmillan Press Ltd. , 2000. Web.

20. Cartmell, Deborah. "Franco Zeffirelli and Shakespeare." Trans. Array *The Cambridge Companion To Shakespeare on Film*. Russel Jackson. Cambridge: Cambridge University Press, 2000. Web.

21. Christ, Henry I. *Shakespeare for the Modern Reader; A User Friendly Introduction*. San Hose, New York, Lincoln, Shanghai: Writer's Showcase , 2002. eBook.

22. Crowl, Samuel. "Looking for Shylock: Stephen Greenblatt, Michael Radford and Al Pacino." Trans. Array*Screening Shakespeare in the Twenty-First Century*. Mark Thornton Burnett and Ramona Wray. Edinburgh: Edinburgh University Press, 2006. Print.

23. Davies, Anthony. *Filming Shakespeare's Plays: The Adaptations of Laurence Olivier, Orson Welles, Peter Brook, and Akira Kurosawa*. Cambridge: Cambridge University Press, 1988. Web.

24.Dessen, Alan C. *Rescripting Shakespeare: The Text, the Director, and Modern Productions.* Cambridge, New York, Melbourne, Madrid, Cape Town: Cambridge University Press, 2002. Web.

25.Emmerich, Roland, dir. *Anonymous.* Perf. Rhys Ifans, Vanessa Redgrave.2011. DVD. Columbia Pictures, Relativity Media;

26.Eyre, Richard, dir. *The Hollow Crown: Henry IV, part I.* Perf. Jeremy Irons as King Henry IV, Simon Russell Beale and Tom Hiddleston. 2012. DVD. British Broadcasting Company (BBC);

27.Eyre, Richard, dir. *The Hollow Crown: Henry IV, part II.* Perf. Jeremy Irons as King Henry IV, Simon Russell Beale and Tom Hiddleston. 2012. DVD. British Broadcasting Company (BBC);

28.Fiennes, Ralph, dir. *Coriolanus.* Perf. Ralph Fiennes, Gerard Butler, Vanessa Redgrave and Brian Cox. 2011. D Films; Lionsgate; The Weinstein Company; Aurum Distribution; British Broadcasting Corporation (BBC).

29.Filling, John."The Body, the Belly and Blood in *Coriolanus*". *From Shakespeare to Brecht through Marx,* a paper presented at the PSA Conference, April 2009. Web.

30. Fischlin , Daniel , and Mark Fortier. *Adaptations of Shakespeare: A critical anthology of plays from the seventeenth century to the present.* 1st ed. London, New York: Routledge, 2000. Web.

31. French, Phllip. "Coriolanus - review." *In his directorial debut Ralph Fiennes has created a vivid, intelligent Coriolanus with powerful political relevance*, 22 01, 2012.

32. Garber, Marjorie. *Shakespeare and Modern Culture.* 1st ed. New York: Anchor Books, 2009. Print.

33. Garber, Marjorie. *Shakespeare After All.* New York: Anchor Books, 2004. Print.

34. Gauntlett, David. *Media, Gender and Identity: an Introduction.* London, New York: Routledge, 2002. eBook.

35. Greenaway, Peter, dir. *Prospero's Books.* Perf. John Gielgud, Michael Clark. 1991. DVD. Allarts; Cine Electra Ltd.

36. Greenblatt, Stephen. *Shakespearian Negotiations: The Circulation of Social Energy in Renaissance England.* 1988. Oxford: Clarendon Press. eBook.

37. Greenblatt, Stephen. *Will in the World.* 2004. New York: Norton. Print.

203

38.Goold, Rupert, dir, *The Hollow Crown: Richard II.* Perf. Ben Whishaw, Rory Kinnear, Patrick Stewart and David Suchet. 2012. DVD; British Broadcasting Company (BBC);

39.Haglund, David. "Is *Coriolanus* Shakespeare's Greatest Tragedy?" 20.1.2012. Web.

40.Hall, Zoe Dare. "Interview With Dragan Micanovic" 20.1.2012.

41.Henderson, Diana E. *A Concise Companion to Shakespeare on Screen.* 1st ed. Malden, Oxford, Victoria, Hong Kong: Blackwell Publishing Ltd, 2006. Print.

42.Heston, Charlton, dir. *Antony and Cleopatra.* Perf. Charlton Heston, Hildegard Niel. 1972. DVD. J. Arthur Rank Film Distributors; 11 Aug 2012

43.Hoffman, Michael, dir. *A Middsummer Night's Dream.* Perf. Kevin Kline, Michelle Pfeiffer, Rupert Everett, Stanley Tucci, Calista Flockhart, Christian Bale, David Strathairn and Sophie Marceau. 1999. DVD. Regency Enterprises; Twentieth Century Fox Film Corporation;

44. Holderness, Graham. *Visual Shakespeare: Essays in Film and Television.* Herfordshire: University of Hertfordshire Press, 2002. eBook.

45. Holderness, Graham. *Cultural Shakespeare: Essays in the Shakespeare Myth.* Herfordshire: University of Hertfordshire Press, 2001. eBook.

46. Hornaday, Ann. "Coriolanus". *A misanthrope for our times.* 17.2.2012.

47. Hoorspool, David. "Coriolanus: Shakespeare's modern political parable". *Ralph Fiennes's new movie adaptation of Shakespeare's political drama is set in the present day and suggests many modern parallels.* 10.1.2012.

48. Jackson, Russel. *The Cambridge Companion to Shakespeare on Film.* 1st ed. Cambridge, New York, Melbourne, Madrid, Cape Town, Singapore, São Paulo: Cambridge University Press, 2000. Web. 8 Nov. 2012

49. Johnston, Trevor. "Coriolanus". *Movie Review from Time Out London,* 19-25 01, 2012.

50.Joughin, John J. *Shakespeare and National Culture*. New York, Manchester: Manchester University Press, 1997. Web. 18 Nov. 2012.

51.Junger, Gil, dir. *10 Things I Hate About You*. Perf. Heath Ledger, Julia Stiles, Joseph Gordon-Levitt and Larry Miller, 1999. DVD. Touchstone Pictures; Buena Vista Pictures;

52.Keller, James R., and Stratyner, Leslie. *Almost Shakespeare: Reinventing His Works for Cinema and Television*. Jefferson: McFarland & Company, Inc., 2004. Web. 10 Nov. 2012.

53.Kennedy, Dennis. *Looking at Shakespeare: A Visual History of Twentieth Century Performance*. 2nd ed. Cambridge: Cambridge University Press, 2001. eBook.

54.Kidnie, Margaret Jane. *Shakespeare and the Problem of Adaptation*. New York: Routledge, 2009. Web. 25. Dec 2012.

55.Kott, Jan. *Shakespeare, Our Contemporary*. Warsaw: PWN (Polish Scientific Publishers). Web. 26 Dec 2012.

56.Kozintzev, Grigori, dir. *Hamlet*. Perf. Innokentiy Smoktunovskiy, Mikhail Nazvanov, Elza Radzina, Yuri Tolubeyev. 1964. DVD. Lenfilm Studio; Palisades Tartan

57. Kozintzev, Grigori, dir. *Korol Lir (King Lear)*. Perf. Jüri Järvet, Elza Radzina and Galina Volchek . 1971. DVD. Lenfilm Studio; Contemporary Films

58. Kurosawa, Akira, dir. *Throne of Blood*. Perf. Toshirô Mifune, Minoru Chiaki and Isuzu Yamada 1957. DVD. Cowboy Pictures; Criterion Collection

59. Kurosawa, Akira, dir. *Ran*. Perf. Tatsuya Nakadai, Akira Terao and Jinpachi Nezu. 1985. DVD. Orion Classics; Criterion Collection.

60. Locraine, Richard, dir. *Richard III*. Perf. Ian McKellen, Annette Bening, Robert Downey, Jr., Kristin Scott Thomas and Jim Broadbent. 1995. DVD. Myfair Entertainment International; United Artists

61. Luhrmann, Baz, dir. *Romeo + Juliet*. Perf. Leonardo DiCaprio, Claire Daines and John Leguizamo. 1996. DVD. Twentieth Century Fox Film Corporation

62. Madden, John, dir. *Shakespeare in Love*. Perf. Joseph Fiennes, Gwyneth Paltrow, Judi Dench, Ben Affleck and Geoffrey Rush. 1998. DVD. Universal Pictures, Miramax Films;

63. Maltin, Leonard. "Coriolanus—movie review." 20 01, 2012.

64. Mankiewicz, Joseph L, dir. *Cleopatra*. Perf. Elizabeth Taylor, Richard Burton and Rex Harrison. 1963. DVD. Twentieth Century Fox Film Corporation

65. Mankiewicz, Joseph L, dir. *Julius Caesar*. Perf. Marlon Brando, Louis Calhern and James Mason. 1953. DVD. Metro-Goldwyn-Meyer (MGM)

66. Martin, Randall, and Katherine Scheil. "Shakespeare Adaptation Modern Drama: Essays in Honour of Jill L. Levenson." Trans. Array *Introduction*. Martin Randall and Katherine Scheil. Toronto, Buffalo, London: University of Toronto Press, 2011. Web.

67. Mason, Pamela. "Orson Welles and Filmed Shakespeare." Trans. Array *The Cambridge Companion To Shakespeare on Film*. Russel Jackson. Cambridge: Cambridge University Press, 2000. Web.

68. Middleton, Alison. "The Art of War" 12. Mar .2012.

69. Moulton, Richard G. "Roman Life: The Ideal of the State in Shakespeare's *Coriolanus*": From: *Shakespeare as a Dramatic Thinker* by Richard G. Moulton. New York, Macmillan 2011. Web.

70. Mueller , Jurgen. *Movies of the 40s*. Los Angeles: TASCHEN, 2005. Print

71. Mueller , Jurgen. *Movies of the 60s*. Los Angeles: TASCHEN, 2003. Print

72. Mueller , Jurgen. *Movies of the 80s*. Los Angeles: TASCHEN, 2003. Print

73. Nelson, Tim Blake, dir. *O*. Perf. Josh Hartnett, Julia Stles, Mekhi Phifer. 2001. DVD. Film Engine; Lions Gate Film.

74. Nunn, Trevor, dir. *Twelfth Night*. Perf. Helena Bonham Carter, Imogen Stubbs and Ben Kingsley. 1996. DVD. BBC Films; Entertainment.

75. Olivier, Laurence, dir. *The Chronicle History of King Henry the Fift with His Battell Fought at Agincourt in France*. Perf. Laurence Olivier, Robert Newton1944. DVD. Two Cities Films; Criterion Collection; Warner Bros. Pictures.

76. Olivier, Laurence, dir. *Hamlet*. Perf. Laurence Olivier, Jean Simmons and John Laurie. 1948. DVD. Two Cities Films; Criterion Collection.

77. Olivier, Laurence, dir *Richard III,* Perf. Laurence Olivier, Cedric Hardwicke and Nicholas Hannen 1955. DVD. MGM Home Entertainment; Criterion Collection.

78. Orgel, Stephen. *The Authentic Shakespeare: And Other Problems on the Early Modern Stage.* New York, London: Routledge. 2002. Web.

79. Pacino, Al, dir. *Looking for Richard.* Perf. Al Pacino, Alec Baldwin, Winona Ryder and Kevin Spacey (1996). DVD. Twentieth Century Fox Film Corporation.

80. Percival, Brian, dir. *Shakespeare Retold: Much Ado About Nothing* . Perf. Sarah Parish, Damian Lewis, Andrew Barclay, George Couyas 2005. DVD. British Broadcasting Corporation (BBC); Horsebridge Productions Limited.

81. Phillips, Michael. "'Coriolanus' on board with Fiennes' ." *Shakespeare's difficult work translates well to modern times,* 02.02. 2012

82. Pittman, Monique L. *Authorizing Shakespeare on Film and Television: Gender, Class and Ethnicity in Adaptation.* New York: Peter Lang Publishing Inc., 2011. eBook.

83.Polanski, Roman, dir. *The Tragedy of Macbeth*. Perf. Jon Finch, Francesca Annis and Martin Shaw 1971. DVD. Playboy Productions; Columbia Pictures.

84.Preston Leonard, Kendra. *Shakspeare, Madness and Music; Scoring Insanity in Cinematic Adaptations* . Lanham, Toronto, Plymouth: The Scarecrow Press, INC., 2009. eBook.

85.Pulver, Andrew. "Coriolanus - review." *Reconfigured as a study of modern warfare, complete with news channel inserts, Ralph Fiennes's directorial debut is a triumph*, 15 02, 2011.

86.Radford, Michael, dir. *The Merchant of Venice*. Perf. Al Pacino, Jeremy Irons, Joseph Fiennes, 2004. DVD. UK Film Council; Sony Pictures Classics

87.Richards, David, dir. *Shakespeare Retold: The Taming of the Shrew*. Shirley Henderson, David Mitchell, Simon Chandler, Jaime Murray 2005. DVD. British Broadcasting Corporation (BBC); Horsebridge Productions Limited.

88.Robbins, Jerome & Wise, Robert, dir. *West Side Story*. 1961. DVD. United Artists; Criterion Collection;

89.Rosenstone, Robert, A. *The Historical Film as Real History*. 2004. Web.

90.Rothwell, Kenneth S. *A History of Shakespeare on Screen: A Century of Film and television*. 2nd. Cambridge: Cambridge University Press, 2004. Web.

91.Schneider, Steven J. *1001 MOVIES you must see before you die* . London: Quintet Publishing, 2003. Print.

92.Scott, A.O. "Dread Rattling Thunder! Yes, It's Shakespeare." 09. Dec. 2010: n. page. Web.

93.Sharock, Thea, dir. *The Hollow Crown: Henry V*. 2012. DVD. Perf. Tom Hiddleston, John Hurt and Geraldine Chaplin. British Broadcasting Company (BBC)

94.Shubert, Amanda. "Undressing: Shakespeare and the Romantic Comedy". 15. Sep. 2012.

95.Sidney, George, dir. *Kiss Me Kate*. Perf. Kathryn Grayson, Howard Keel and Ann Miller 1953. DVD. Metro-Goldwyn-Meyer (MGM)

96.Sokolyanski, Mark. "Grigori Kozintzev's Hamlet and King Lear." Trans. Array *The Cambridge Companion To Shakespeare on*

Film. Russel Jackson. Cambridge: Cambridge University Press, 2000. Web.

97. Spicci, Mauro. "The body as metaphor: digestive bodies and political surgery in Shakespeare's *Macbeth*". Published online in J Med Ethics; Medical Humanities 2007;33:67–69. doi: 10.1136/jmh.2007.000257.

98. Stanley, Alessandra. "Timeless Tales With a Modern Twist in 'ShakespeaRe-Told'". 6.8.2006. Web.

99. Starks, Lisa S., and Lehmann Courtney. "Images of the ." Trans. Array *The Reel Shakespeare*. Lisa S. Starks and Courtney Lehmann. Cranbury, London, Mississauga: Rosemont Publishing and Printing Corp., 2002. Web

100. Taylor, Samuel, dir. *The Taming of the Shrew*. Perf. Mary Pickford, Douglas Fairbanks. 1929. DVD. Elton Corporation; United Artists;

101. Taymor, Julie, dir. *Titus*. Perf. Anthony Hopkins, Jessica Lange and Osheen Jones. 1999. DVD. Clear Blue Sky Productions; Fox Searchlight Pictures.

102.   Taymor, Julie, dir. *The Tempest* Perf. Hellen Mirren, Alfred Molina, Russel Brand, Ben Whishaw and Djimon Honsou. 2010. DVD. Miramax Films; Touchstone Pictures;

103.   Trayler, Helen, ed. *The Complete Works of William Shakespeare.* London: Wordsworth Editions Limited, 2007. Print.

104.   Van Sant, Gus, dir. *My Own Private Idaho.* Perf. Keanu Reeves, River Phoenix and James Russo. 1991. DVD. New Line Cinema; Criterion Collection;

105.   Walker, Elsie, and . Trans. Array *The Literature/Film Reader: Issues of Adaption.* James M. Wels and Peter Lev. Lanham, Toronto, Plymouth: The Scarecrow Press, INC., 2003. Web.

106.   Welles, Orson, dir. *Macbeth.* Orson Welles, Jeanette Nolan and Dan O'Herlihy 1948. DVD. Republic Pictures; Criterion Collection

107.   Welles, Orson, dir. *Othello.* Orson Welles, Micheál MacLiammóir and Robert Coote. 1952. DVD. United Artists; Criterion Collection

108.   Welles, Orson, dir. *Chimes at Midnight.* Perf. Orson Welles, Jeanne   Moreau,   keith   Baxter,   John

Gielgud and Margaret Rutherford 1966. DVD. Alpine Films; Planet.

109.   Welsh, James M., and Peter M. Lev. ed. *The Literature/Film Reader: Issues of Adaption*. Lanham, Toronto, Plymouth: The Scarecrow Press, INC., 2007. Print.

110.   Wise, David. "Anonymous – review The shock in this exposé of the Bard is that it's rather good." 10 Nov 2011: n. page. Print.

111.   Worthen, W.B. *Shakespeare and the Force of Modern Performance* . 1st ed. Cambridge: Cambridge University Press, 2003. Web.

112.   Zeffirelli, Franco, dir. *The Taming of the Shrew.* Perf. Elizabeth Taylor, Richard Burton and Cyril Cusack 1967. DVD. Columbia Pictures; Clombia TriStar

113.   Zeffirelli, Franco, dir. *Romeo and Juliet.* Perf. Leonard Whiting, Olivia Hussey and John McEnery 1968. DVD. Paramount Pictures

114. Zeffirelli, Franco, dir. *Hamlet.* Perf. Mel Gibson, Glenn Close, Ian Holm, Helena Bonham Carter and Alan Bates.1990. DVD. Warner Bros.

115. Zupančič, Alenka. *The Odd One In: On Comedy.* Cambridge, Massachusetts: The MIT Press. 2008. Print.

i want morebooks!

Buy your books fast and straightforward online - at one of world's fastest growing online book stores! Environmentally sound due to Print-on-Demand technologies.

Buy your books online at
www.get-morebooks.com

Kaufen Sie Ihre Bücher schnell und unkompliziert online – auf einer der am schnellsten wachsenden Buchhandelsplattformen weltweit! Dank Print-On-Demand umwelt- und ressourcenschonend produziert.

Bücher schneller online kaufen
www.morebooks.de

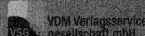 VDM Verlagsservicegesellschaft mbH
Heinrich-Böcking-Str. 6-8   Telefon: +49 681 3720 174   info@vdm-vsg.de
D - 66121 Saarbrücken   Telefax: +49 681 3720 1749   www.vdm-vsg.de

Printed in Great Britain
by Amazon

57613451R00129